scar

pattern on page 35

clash

pattern on page 47

yoyo

pattern on page 40

skulk

pattern on page 43

pattern on page 40

knot

pattern on page 32

dreads
pattern on page 38

skruff
pattern on page 43

TRUCK HERE
benchmark
WEIGHT 45Kg GROSS
WALL MOUNTED
GAS-FIRED
SYSTEM BOILER
SUPER DISCOUNT

dreads

pattern on page 38

fresh stuff

pattern on page 36

pattern on page 43

quirk

pattern on page 50

pattern on page 50

pattern on page 53

DIABOLICAL

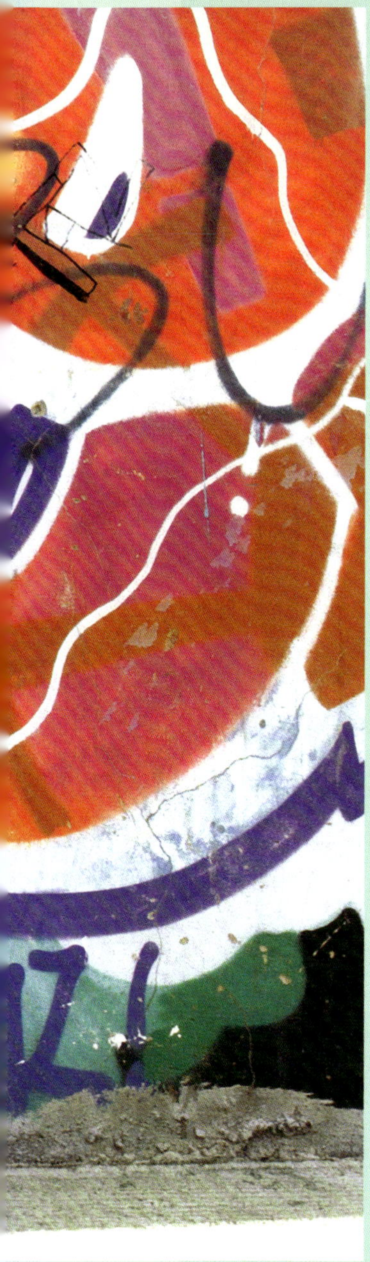

lusty

pattern on page 53

beat

pattern on page 45

rare

pattern on page 52

rare

pattern on page 52

curious doll

pattern on page 34

moody

pattern on page 43

VIZO..
.TAME

scream clash

pattern on page 37

pattern on page 47

sassy

pattern on page 44

venus

pattern on page 41

index

No. 1

KOOK

YARN

	XS	S	M	L	XL	
To fit bust	81	86	91	97	102	cm
	32	34	36	38	40	in

Rowan Spray, Big Wool and Wool Cotton

A Spray Calm 007

8	8	9	9	10	x100gm

B Big WoolLatte 018

1	1	1	1	1	x100gm

C W CottDream 929

1	1	1	1	1	x50gm

NEEDLES

1 pair 4mm (no 8) (US 6) needles
1 pair 8mm (no 0) (US 11) needles
1 pair 10mm (no 000) (US 15) needles

ZIPS – 2 x 15 cm zips (for pockets), and open-ended zip to fit

TENSION

9 sts and 11 rows to 10 cm measured over stocking stitch using 10mm (US 15) needles.

BACK

Using 8mm (US 11) needles and yarn A cast on 46 [48: 50: 54: 56] sts.
Row 1 (RS): P0 [1: 2: 0: 1], *K2, P2, rep from * to last 2 [3: 0: 2: 3] sts, K2 [2: 0: 2: 2], P0 [1: 0: 0: 1].
Row 2: K0 [1: 2: 0: 1], *P2, K2, rep from * to last 2 [3: 0: 2: 3] sts, P2 [2: 0: 2: 2], K0 [1: 0: 0: 1].
These 2 rows form rib.
Work in rib for a further 3 rows, ending with **WS** facing for next row.
Change to 10mm (US 15) needles.
Beg with a **P** row, work in st st until back meas 19 [20: 20: 21: 21] cm, ending with RS facing for next row.
Next row (dec) (RS): K2, sl 1, K1, psso, K to last 4 sts, K2tog, K2.
Working all side seam decreases as set by last row, dec 1 st at each end of 4th and every foll 6th row until 38 [40: 42: 46: 48] sts rem.
Work 5 rows, ending with RS facing for next row.
Next row (inc) (RS): K2, M1, K to last 2 sts, M1, K2.
Working all side seam increases as set by last row, inc 1 st at each end of 6th row.
42 [44: 46: 50: 52] sts.
Cont straight until back meas 58 [59: 59: 60: 60] cm, ending with RS facing for next row.

Shape armholes

Cast off 3 sts at beg of next 2 rows.
36 [38: 40: 44: 46] sts.
Dec 1 st at each end of next 3 [3: 4: 5: 6] rows.
30 [32: 32: 34: 34] sts.
Cont straight until armhole meas 21 [21: 22: 22: 23] cm, ending with RS facing for next row.

Shape shoulders

Cast off 7 [8: 8: 8: 8] sts at beg of next 2 rows.
Break yarn and leave rem 16 [16: 16: 18: 18] sts on a holder.

LEFT FRONT

Using 8mm (US 11) needles and yarn A cast on 23 [24: 25: 27: 28] sts.
Row 1 (RS): P0 [1: 2: 0: 1], *K2, P2, rep from * to last 3 sts, K2, P1.
Row 2: K1, *P2, K2, rep from * to last 2 [3: 0: 2: 3] sts, P2 [2: 0: 2: 2], K0 [1: 0: 0: 1].
These 2 rows form rib.
Work in rib for a further 3 rows, ending with **WS** facing for next row.
Change to 10mm (US 15) needles.
Beg with a **P** row, work in st st until left front meas 19 [20: 20: 21: 21] cm, ending with RS facing for next row.
Next row (dec) (RS): K2, sl 1, K1, psso, K to end.
Working all side seam decreases as set by last row, dec 1 st at beg of 4th row.
21 [22: 23: 25: 26] sts.
Work 3 rows, ending with RS facing for next row.

Place pocket opening

Next row (RS): K4 [5: 6: 6: 7], cast off next 12 sts, K to end.
Next row: Purl, casting on 12 sts over those cast off on previous row.
Dec 1 st at beg of next and foll 6th row.
19 [20: 21: 23: 24] sts.
Work 5 rows, ending with RS facing for next row.
Next row (inc) (RS): K2, M1, K to end.
Working all side seam increases as set by last row, inc 1 st at beg of 6th row.
21 [22: 23: 25: 26] sts.
Cont straight until left front matches back to beg of armhole shaping,

ending with RS facing for next row.

Shape armhole

Cast off 3 sts at beg of next row.
18 [19: 20: 22: 23] sts.
Work 1 row.
Dec 1 st at armhole edge of next 3 [3: 4: 5: 6] rows.
15 [16: 16: 17: 17] sts.
Cont straight until 5 rows less have been worked than on back to beg of shoulder shaping, ending with **WS** facing for next row.

Shape neck

Cast off 6 [6: 6: 7: 7] sts at beg of next row.
9 [10: 10: 10: 10] sts.
Dec 1 st at neck edge of next 2 rows.
7 [8: 8: 8: 8] sts.
Work 2 rows, ending with RS facing for next row.

Shape shoulder

Cast off.

RIGHT FRONT

Using 8mm (US 11) needles and yarn A cast on 23 [24: 25: 27: 28] sts.
Row 1 (RS): P1, *K2, P2, rep from * to last 2 [3: 0: 2: 3] sts, K2 [2: 0: 2: 2], P0 [1: 0: 0: 1].
Row 2: K0 [1: 2: 0: 1], *P2, K2, rep from * to last 3 sts, P2, K1.
These 2 rows form rib.
Work in rib for a further 3 rows, ending with **WS** facing for next row.
Change to 10mm (US 15) needles.
Beg with a **P** row, work in st st until right front meas 19 [20: 20: 21: 21] cm, ending with RS facing for next row.
Next row (dec) (RS): K to last 4 sts, K2tog, K2.
Working all side seam decreases as set by last row, dec 1 st at end of 4th row.
21 [22: 23: 25: 26] sts.
Work 3 rows, ending with RS facing for next row.

Place pocket opening

Next row (RS): K5 [5: 5: 7: 7], cast off next 12 sts, K to end.
Next row: Purl, casting on 12 sts over those cast off on previous row.
Complete to match left front, reversing shapings, working an extra row before beg of armhole, neck and shoulder shaping.

SLEEVES

Using 8mm (US 11) needles and yarn A cast on 22 [22: 24: 24: 26] sts.
Row 1 (RS): K0 [0: 1: 1: 0], *P2, K2, rep from * to last 2 [2: 3: 3: 2] sts, P2, K0 [0: 1: 1: 0].
Row 2: P0 [0: 1: 1: 0], *K2, P2, rep from * to last 2 [2: 3: 3: 2] sts, K2, P0 [0: 1: 1: 0].
These 2 rows form rib.
Work in rib for a further 4 rows, ending with RS facing for next row.
Change to 10mm (US 15) needles.
Cont in rib, inc 1 st at each end of 7th row.
24 [24: 26: 26: 28] sts.
Work 1 row, ending with RS facing for next row.
Beg with a K row, work in st st, shaping sides by inc 1 st at each end of 5th and every foll 6th row to 32 [32: 34: 34: 36] sts, then on foll 8th row.
34 [34: 36: 36: 38] sts.
Cont straight until sleeve meas 45 [45: 46: 46: 46] cm, ending with RS facing for next row.

Shape top

Cast off 3 sts at beg of next 2 rows.
28 [28: 30: 30: 32] sts.
Dec 1 st at each end of next 3 rows, then on every foll alt row until 12 sts rem, then on foll row, ending with RS facing for next row.
Cast off rem 10 sts.

MAKING UP

Press as described on the information page.
Join shoulder seams using back stitch, or mattress stitch if preferred.

Neckband

With RS facing, using 8mm (US 11) needles and yarn A, pick up and knit 11 [11: 11: 12: 12] sts up right side of neck, K16 [16: 16: 18: 18] sts from back, then pick up and knit 11 [11: 11: 12: 12] sts down left side of neck.
38 [38: 38: 42: 42] sts.
Row 1 (WS): P2, *K2, P2, rep from * to end.
Row 2: K2, *P2, K2, rep from * to end.
Rep last 2 rows until neckband meas 9 cm.
Cast off in rib.

Front bands (both alike)

With RS facing, using 8mm (US 11) needles and yarn B, pick up and knit 76 [77: 78: 79: 80] sts along front opening edge, between pick-up row for neckband and cast-on edge.
Cast off knitwise (on **WS**).

Pocket linings (make 2)

Using 4mm (US 6) needles and yarn C cast on 28 sts.
Beg with a K row, work in st st for 15 cm, ending with RS facing for next row.
Cast off.
See information page for finishing instructions, setting in sleeves using the set-in method.
Insert zips into pocket openings, then sew pocket linings in place over zips on inside.

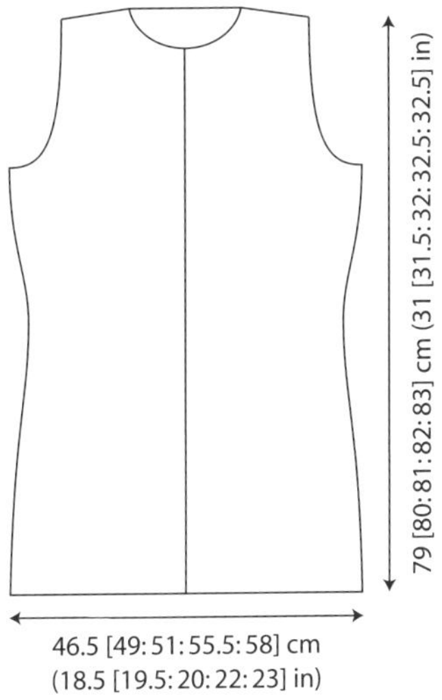

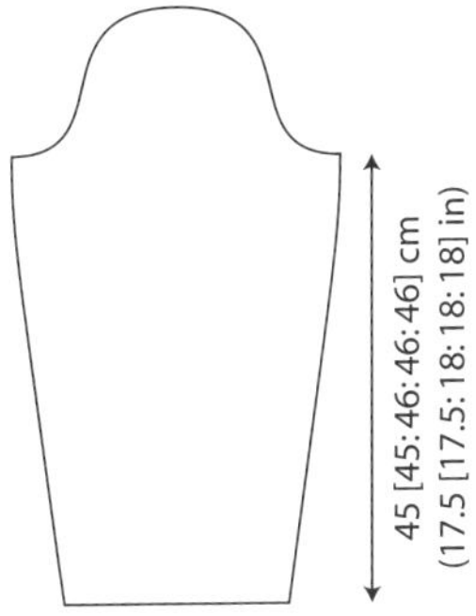

No. 2

CURIOUS DOLL

YARN

	XS	S	M	L	XL	
To fit bust	81	86	91	97	102	cm
	32	34	36	38	40	in

Rowan Spray and Kid Classic

	XS	S	M	L	XL	
A Spray Sunset 004	6	7	7	8	8	x100gm
B Kid P Sorbet 842	1	1	1	1	1	x50gm
C Kid Feather 828	1	1	1	1	1	x50gm
D Kid Frilly 844	1	1	1	1	1	x50gm

NEEDLES

1 pair 10mm (no 000) (US 15) needles

TENSION

9 sts and 11 rows to 10 cm measured over stocking stitch using 10mm (US 15) needles.

BACK

Using 10mm (US 15) needles and yarn A cast on 53 [55: 57: 61: 63] sts.

Row 1 (RS): K1, *P1, K1, rep from * to end.

Row 2: P1, *K1, P1, rep from * to end.

These 2 rows form rib.

Work in rib for a further 2 rows, dec 1 st at end of last row and ending with RS facing for next row.

52 [54: 56: 60: 62] sts.

Beg with a K row, work in st st for 6 rows, ending with RS facing for next row.

Row 7 (RS): K1, sl 1, K1, psso, K to last 3 sts, K2tog, K1.

Working all side seam decreases as set by last row, dec 1 st at each end of every foll 4th row until 38 [40: 42: 46: 48] sts rem.

Cont straight until back meas 40 [41: 41: 42: 42] cm, ending with RS facing for next row.

Shape armholes

Dec 1 st at each end of next 4 rows.

30 [32: 34: 38: 40] sts.

Cont straight until armhole meas 20 [20: 21: 21: 22] cm, ending with RS facing for next row.

Shape shoulders

Cast off 2 [3: 3: 4: 4] sts at beg of next 2 rows, then 3 [3: 4: 4: 5] sts at beg of foll 2 rows.

Break yarn and leave rem 20 [20: 20: 22: 22] sts on a holder.

FRONT

Work as given for back until 18 rows less have been worked than on back to beg of shoulder shaping, ending with RS facing for next row.

Shape neck

Next row (RS): K10 [11: 12: 13: 14] and turn, leaving rem sts on a holder.

Work each side of neck separately.

Dec 1 st at neck edge of next and foll 3 alt rows, then on foll 4th row.

5 [6: 7: 8: 9] sts.

Work 6 rows, ending with RS facing for next row.

Shape shoulder

Cast off 2 [3: 3: 4: 4] sts at beg of next row.

Work 1 row.

Cast off rem 3 [3: 4: 4: 5] sts.

With RS facing, slip centre 10 [10: 10: 12: 12] sts onto a holder, rejoin yarn to rem sts, K to end.

Complete to match first side, reversing shapings.

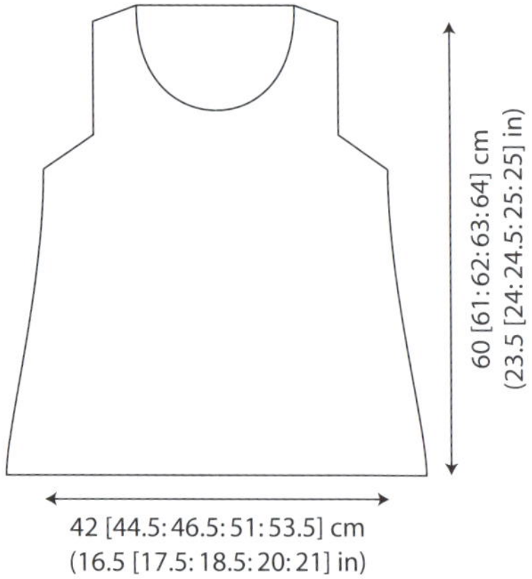

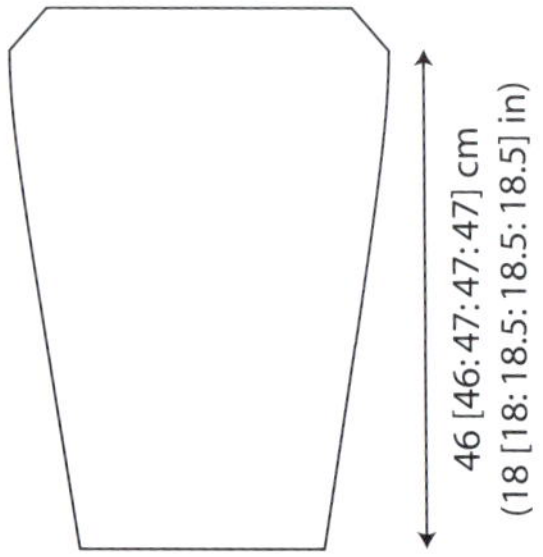

SLEEVES
Using 10mm (US 15) needles cast on 27 [27: 29: 29: 31] sts.
Work in rib as given for back for 4 rows, ending with RS facing for next row.
Beg with a K row, work in st st, shaping sides by inc 1 st at each end of 5th and every foll 12th row until there are 35 [35: 37: 37: 39] sts.
Cont straight until sleeve meas 46 [46: 47: 47: 47] cm, ending with RS facing for next row.

Shape top
Dec 1 st at each end of next 4 rows, ending with RS facing for next row.
Cast off rem 27 [27: 29: 29: 31] sts.

MAKING UP
Press as described on the information page.
Join right shoulder seam using back stitch, or mattress stitch if preferred.

Collar
With RS facing and using 10mm (US 15) needles, pick up and knit 18 sts down left side of neck, K10 [10: 10: 12: 12] sts from front, pick up and knit 17 sts up right side of neck, then K20 [20: 20: 22: 22] sts from back. 65 [65: 65: 69: 69] sts.
Beg with a P row, work in st st for 8cm, ending with RS facing for next row.
Work in rib as given for back for 4 rows, ending with RS facing for next row.
Cast off in rib.
See information page for finishing instructions, setting in sleeves using the shallow set-in method.
Using photograph as a guide, embroider front and sleeves of sweater as folls: Twist tog 2 strands each of yarns B, C and D and form into spiral shapes. Oversew in place using yarn B.

No. 3
SCAR

YARN
Rowan Spray
2 x 100gm
(photographed in Mellow 002)

NEEDLES
1 pair 10mm (no 000) (US 15) needles

BUTTONS – 3 x 00355

FINISHED SIZE
Completed scarf measures 16 cm (6½in) wide and 89 cm (35 in) long.

TENSION
9 sts and 11 rows to 10 cm measured over stocking stitch using 10mm (US 15) needles.

SCARF
Using 10mm (US 15) needles cast on 2 sts.
Row 1 (RS): Inc once in each st. 4 sts.
Row 2: K1, P2, K1.
Row 3: Inc in first st, K to last 2 sts, inc in next st, K1. 6 sts.
Row 4: K1, P to last st, K1.
Rows 5 to 12: As rows 3 and 4, 4 times. 14 sts.
Row 13: Knit.
Row 14: K1, P to last st, K1.
Last 2 rows form patt.
Cont in patt until scarf meas 85 cm, ending with RS facing for next row.
Next row (RS): (K2, yfwd, K2tog) 3 times, K2.
Patt a further 2 rows, ending with **WS** facing for next row.
Next row (WS): Knit (to form fold line).
Cont in patt until scarf meas 14 cm **from fold line row**, ending with RS facing for next row.
Cast off.

MAKING UP
Press as described on the information page.
Fold cast-off edge to WS along fold line row and sew cast-off edge in place on WS. Sew on buttons.

No. 4

FRESH

YARN

	XS	S	M	L	XL	
To fit bust	81	86	91	97	102	cm
	32	34	36	38	40	in

Rowan Spray

6	7	7	8	8	x100gm

(photographed in Seascape 006)

NEEDLES

1 pair 8mm (no 0) (US 11) needles
1 pair 10mm (no 000) (US 15) needles

TENSION

9 sts and 11 rows to 10 cm measured over stocking stitch using 10mm (US 15) needles.

BACK

Using 8mm (US 11) needles cast on 41 [43: 45: 49: 51] sts.

Row 1 (RS): K1, *P1, K1, rep from * to end.

Row 2: P1, *K1, P1, rep from * to end.

These 2 rows form rib.

Change to 10mm (US 15) needles.

Row 1 (RS): K0 [1: 2: 0: 0], P2 [2: 2: 1: 2], (K3, P2) 2 [2: 2: 3: 3] times, K4, P2, K5, P2, K4, (P2, K3) 2 [2: 2: 3: 3] times, P2 [2: 2: 1: 2], K0 [1: 2: 0: 0].

Row 2: P0 [1: 2: 0: 0], K2 [2: 2: 1: 2], (P3, K2) 2 [2: 2: 3: 3] times, P4, K2, P5, K2, P4, (K2, P3) 2 [2: 2: 3: 3] times, K2 [2: 2: 1: 2], P0 [1: 2: 0: 0].

These 2 rows form patt.

Cont in patt until back meas 37 [38: 38: 39: 39] cm, ending with RS facing for next row.

Shape armholes

Keeping patt correct, dec 1 st at each end of next 4 rows. 33 [35: 37: 41: 43] sts.

Cont straight until armhole meas 20 [20: 21: 21: 22] cm, ending with RS facing for next row.

Shape shoulders

Cast off 4 [5: 5: 6: 6] sts at beg of next 2 rows, then 5 [5: 6: 6: 7] sts at beg of foll 2 rows.

Break yarn and leave rem 15 [15: 15: 17: 17] sts on a holder.

FRONT

Work as given for back until 2 rows less have been worked than on back to beg of shoulder shaping, ending with RS facing for next row.

Shape neck

Next row (RS): Patt 11 [12: 13: 14: 15] sts and turn, leaving rem sts on a holder.

Work each side of neck separately.

Dec 1 st at neck edge of next row, ending with RS facing for next row. 10 [11: 12: 13: 14] sts.

Shape shoulder

Cast off 4 [5: 5: 6: 6] sts at beg and dec 1 st at end of next row.

Work 1 row.

Cast off rem 5 [5: 6: 6: 7] sts.

With RS facing, slip centre 11 [11: 11: 13: 13] sts onto a holder, rejoin yarn to rem sts, patt to end.

Complete to match first side, reversing shapings.

SLEEVES

Using 8mm (US 11) needles cast on 19 [19: 21: 21: 23] sts.

Work in rib as given for back for 2 rows, ending with RS facing for next row.

Change to 10mm (US 15) needles.

Row 1 (RS): K0 [0: 1: 1: 2], P2, K3,

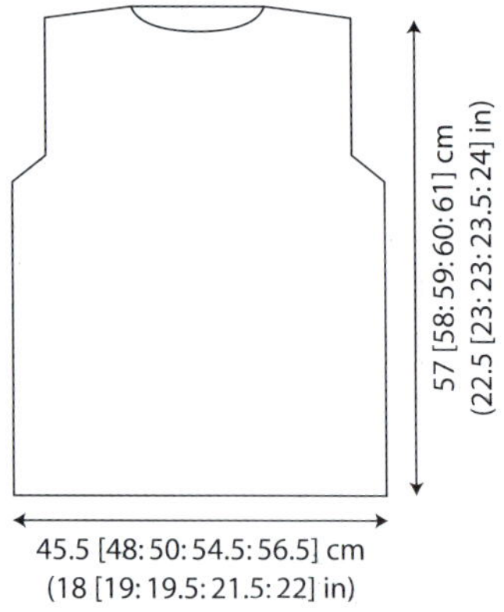

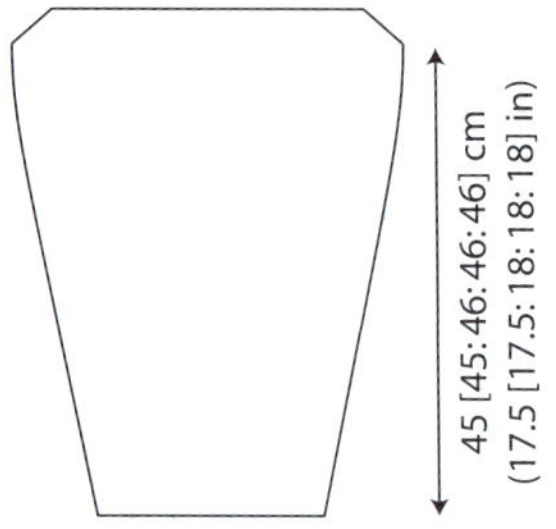

P2, K5, P2, K3, P2, K0 [0: 1: 1: 2].
Row 2: P0 [0: 1: 1: 2], K2, P3, K2, P5, K2, P3, K2, P0 [0: 1: 1: 2].
These 2 rows form patt.
Cont in patt, shaping sides by inc 1 st at each end of next and every foll 4th [4th: 6th: 6th: 6th] row to 23 [23: 37: 37: 39] sts, then on every foll 6th [6th: -: -: -] row until there are 35 [35: -: -: -] sts, taking inc sts into patt.
Cont straight until sleeve meas 45 [45: 46: 46: 46] cm, ending with RS facing for next row.

Shape top
Keeping patt correct, dec 1 st at each end of next 4 rows, ending with RS facing for next row.
Cast off rem 27 [27: 29: 29: 31] sts.

MAKING UP
Press as described on the information page.
Join right shoulder seam using back stitch, or mattress stitch if preferred.

Neckband
With RS facing and using 8mm (US 11) needles, pick up and knit 5 sts down left side of neck, patt 11 [11: 11: 13: 13] sts from front, pick up and knit 4 sts up right side of neck, then patt 15 [15: 15: 17: 17] sts from back. 35 [35: 35: 39: 39] sts.
Row 1 (WS): P3 [3: 3: 4: 4], K2, P5, K2, (P3 [3: 3: 4: 4], K2) twice, P5, K2, P3 [3: 3: 4: 4], K2, P1.
Row 2: K1, P2, K3 [3: 3: 4: 4], P2, K5, P2, (K3 [3: 3: 4: 4], P2) twice, K5, P2, K3 [3: 3: 4: 4].
Rows 3 to 8: As rows 1 and 2, 3 times.
Work in rib as given for back for 2 rows, ending with **WS** facing for next row.
Cast off in rib (on **WS**).
See information page for finishing instructions, setting in sleeves using the shallow set-in method.

No. 5

SCREAM

YARN
Rowan Spray
3 x 100gm
(photographed in Sensation 008)

NEEDLES
1 pair 10mm (no 000) (US 15) needles

FINISHED SIZE
Completed scarf measures 18 cm (7 in) wide and 160 cm (63 in) long.

TENSION
9 sts and 11 rows to 10 cm measured over stocking stitch using 10mm (US 15) needles.

SCARF
Using 10mm (US 15) needles cast on 16 sts.
Rows 1 and 2: Knit.
Row 3 (RS): K6, (yfwd) twice, K1, (yfwd) 3 times, K1, (yfwd) 4 times, K1, (yfwd) 3 times, K1, (yfwd) twice, K6.
Row 4: K to end, dropping all yfwd's of previous row.
16 sts.
Rows 5 and 6: Knit.
Row 7: K1, *(yfwd) twice, K1, (yfwd) 3 times, K1, (yfwd) 4 times, K1, (yfwd) 3 times, K1, (yfwd) twice*, K6, rep from * to * once more, K1.
Row 8: As row 4.
These 8 rows form patt.
Cont in patt until scarf meas approx 160 cm, ending after patt row 2 or 6 and with RS facing for next row.
Cast off.

MAKING UP
Press as described on the information page.

No. 6

DREADS

YARN

	XS	S	M	L	XL	
To fit bust	81	86	91	97	102	cm
	32	34	36	38	40	in

Rowan Spray

Longer version

7	7	8	8	9	x100gm

(photographed in Calm 007)

Shorter version

6	6	6	7	7	x100gm

(photographed in Mood 005)

NEEDLES

1 pair 8mm (no 0) (US 11) needles
1 pair 10mm (no 000) (US 15) needles

DECORATION – Longer version only:

1 x 50g ball of Rowan Wool Cotton in Coffee Rich 956. 5 x large, 15 x medium and 10 x small buttons

TENSION

9 sts and 11 rows to 10 cm measured over stocking stitch using 10mm (US 15) needles.

Longer version

BACK

Using 8mm (US 11) needles cast on 43 [45: 47: 51: 53] sts.

Row 1 (RS): K1, *P1, K1, rep from * to end.

Row 2: P1, *K1, P1, rep from * to end.

These 2 rows form rib.

Work in rib for a further 4 rows, ending with RS facing for next row.

Change to 10mm (US 15) needles.

Beg with a K row, work in st st for 6 rows, ending with RS facing for next row.

Row 7 (dec) (RS): K1, sl 1, K1, psso, K to last 3 sts, K2tog, K1.

Work 11 rows.

Row 19: As row 7.

39 [41: 43: 47: 49] sts.

Cont straight until back meas 39 [40: 40: 41: 41] cm, ending with RS facing for next row.

Shape armholes

Cast off 2 sts at beg of next 2 rows.

35 [37: 39: 43: 45] sts.

Dec 1 st at each end of next 3 [4: 4: 6: 6] rows. 29 [29: 31: 31: 33] sts.

Cont straight until armhole meas 20 [20: 21: 21: 22] cm, ending with RS facing for next row.

Shape shoulders

Cast off 7 [7: 8: 7: 8] sts at beg of next 2 rows.

Break yarn and leave rem 15 [15: 15: 17: 17] sts on a holder.

FRONT

Work as given for back until 6 rows less have been worked than on back to beg of shoulder shaping, ending with RS facing for next row.

Shape neck

Next row (RS): K10 [10: 11: 10: 11] and turn, leaving rem sts on a holder.

Work each side of neck separately.

Dec 1 st at neck edge of next 3 rows.

7 [7: 8: 7: 8] sts.

Work 2 rows, ending with RS facing for next row.

Shape shoulder

Cast off.

With RS facing, slip centre 9 [9: 9: 11: 11] sts onto a holder, rejoin yarn to rem sts, K to end.

Complete to match first side, reversing shapings.

SLEEVES

Using 8mm (US 11) needles cast on 19 [19: 21: 21: 23] sts.

Work in rib as given for back for 4 rows, ending with RS facing for next row.

Change to 10mm (US 15) needles.

Beg with a K row, work in st st, shaping sides by inc 1 st at each end of 3rd [3rd: 5th: 5th: 5th] and every foll 6th row until there are 33 [33: 35: 35: 37] sts.

Cont straight until sleeve meas 45 [45: 46: 46: 46] cm, ending with RS facing for next row.

Shape top

Cast off 2 sts at beg of next 2 rows.

29 [29: 31: 31: 33] sts.

Dec 1 st at each end of next 3 rows, then on every foll alt row until 17 sts rem, then on foll 3 rows, ending with RS facing for next row.

Cast off rem 11 sts.

MAKING UP
Press as described on the information page.
Join right shoulder seam using back stitch, or mattress stitch if preferred.

Neckband
With RS facing and using 8mm (US 11) needles, pick up and knit 5 sts down left side of neck, K9 [9: 9: 11: 11] sts from front, pick up and knit 4 sts up right side of neck, then K15 [15: 15: 17: 17] sts from back.
33 [33: 33: 37: 37] sts.
Beg with row 2, work in rib as given for back for 6 cm.
Change to 10mm (US 15) needles.
Cont in rib until neckband meas 9 cm, ending with RS facing for next row.
Cast off in rib.
See information page for finishing instructions, setting in sleeves using the set-in method.
Using photograph as a guide and Wool Cotton, embroider chain st 10 pointed "snowflake" design onto front.
Attach buttons as in photograph.

Shorter version

BACK
Using 8mm (US 11) needles cast on 39 [41: 43: 47: 49] sts.
Row 1 (RS): K1, *P1, K1, rep from * to end.
Row 2: P1, *K1, P1, rep from * to end.
These 2 rows form rib.
Work in rib for a further 4 rows, ending with RS facing for next row.
Change to 10mm (US 15) needles.
Beg with a K row, work in st st until back meas 31 [32: 32: 33: 33] cm, ending with RS facing for next row.
Complete as given for back of longer version from beg of armhole shaping.

FRONT
Work as given for back until 8 rows less have been worked than on back to beg of shoulder shaping, ending with RS facing for next row.

Shape neck
Next row (RS): K12 [12: 13: 12: 13] and turn, leaving rem sts on a holder.
Work each side of neck separately.
Dec 1 st at neck edge of next 5 rows.
7 [7: 8: 7: 8] sts.
Work 2 rows, ending with RS facing for next row.

Shape shoulder
Cast off.
With RS facing, slip centre 5 [5: 5: 7: 7] sts onto a holder, rejoin yarn to rem sts, K to end.
Complete to match first side, reversing shapings.

SLEEVES
Work as given for sleeves of longer version.

MAKING UP
Press as described on the information page.
Join right shoulder seam using back stitch, or mattress stitch if preferred.

Neckband
With RS facing and using 8mm (US 11) needles, pick up and knit 7 sts down left side of neck, K5 [5: 5: 7: 7] sts from front, pick up and knit 6 sts up right side of neck, then K15 [15: 15: 17: 17] sts from back.
33 [33: 33: 37: 37] sts.
Beg with row 2, work in rib as given for back for 4 rows, ending with **WS** facing for next row.
Cast off in rib (on **WS**).
See information page for finishing instructions, setting in sleeves using the set-in method.

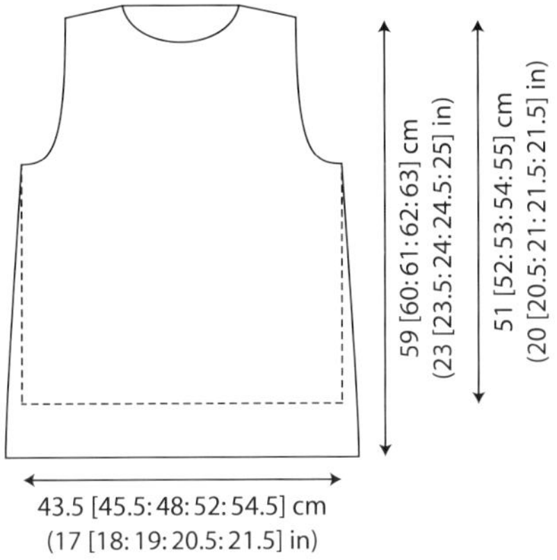

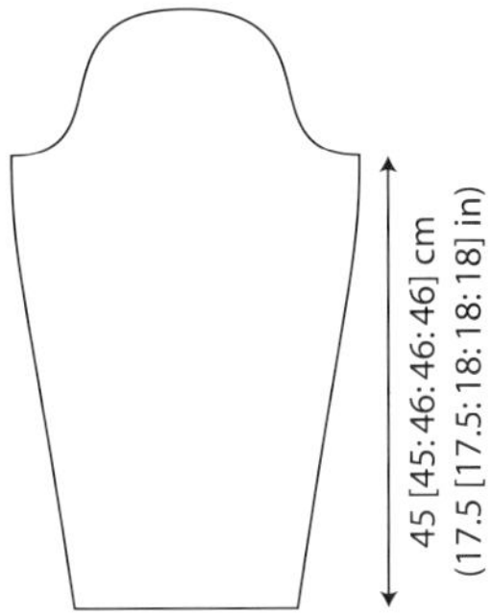

No. 7

YO-YO

YARN

	XS	S	M	L	XL	
To fit bust	81	86	91	97	102	cm
	32	34	36	38	40	in

Rowan Spray

5	6	6	6	7	x100gm

(photographed in Mood 005)

NEEDLES

1 pair 8mm (no 0) (US 11) needles
1 pair 10mm (no 000) (US 15) needles

TENSION

8 sts and 10 rows to 10 cm measured over pattern using 10mm (US 15) needles.

BACK

Using 10mm (US 15) needles cast on 36 [38: 40: 42: 44] sts.

Row 1 (RS): K1, *yfwd, sl 1, K1, psso, rep from * to last st, K1.

Row 2: P1, *yrn, P2tog, rep from * to last st, P1.

These 2 rows form patt.

Cont in patt until back meas 31 [32: 32: 33: 33] cm, ending with RS facing for next row.

Shape armholes

Keeping patt correct, dec 1 st at each end of next 4 rows. 28 [30: 32: 34: 36] sts.

Cont straight until armhole meas 20 [20: 21: 21: 22] cm, ending with RS facing for next row.

Shape shoulders

Cast off 7 [8: 9: 9: 10] sts at beg of next 2 rows.

Break yarn and leave rem 14 [14: 14: 16: 16] sts on a holder.

FRONT

Work as given for back until 4 rows less have been worked than on back to beg of shoulder shaping, ending with RS facing for next row.

Shape neck

Next row (RS): Patt 9 [10: 11: 11: 12] sts and turn, leaving rem sts on a holder.

Work each side of neck separately.

Dec 1 st at neck edge of next 2 rows. 7 [8: 9: 9: 10] sts.

Work 1 row, ending with RS facing for next row.

Shape shoulder

Cast off.

With RS facing, slip centre 10 [10: 10: 12: 12] sts onto a holder, rejoin yarn to rem sts, patt to end.

Complete to match first side, reversing shapings.

SLEEVES

Using 10mm (US 15) needles cast on 16 [16: 18: 18: 20] sts.

Work in patt as given for back, shaping sides by inc 1 st at each end of 3rd [3rd: 5th: 5th: 5th] and every foll 6th row until there are 30 [30: 32: 32: 34] sts, taking inc sts into patt.

Cont straight until sleeve meas 45 [45: 46: 46: 46] cm, ending with RS facing for next row.

Shape top

Keeping patt correct, dec 1 st at each end of next 4 rows, ending

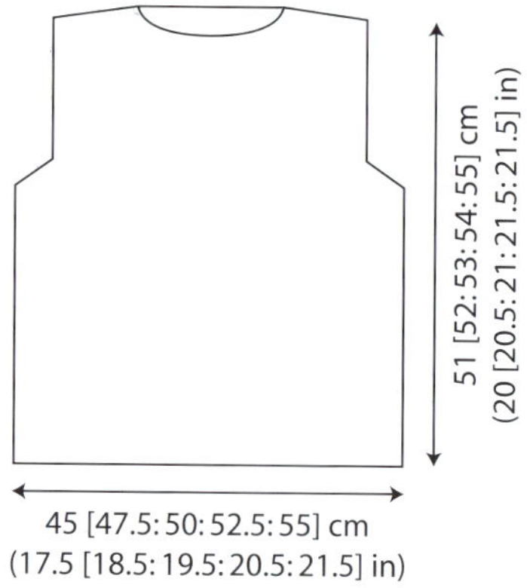

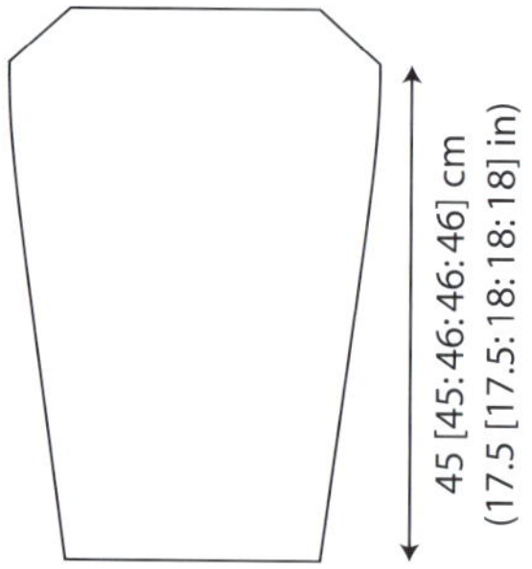

with RS facing for next row.
Cast off rem 22 [22: 24: 24: 26] sts.

MAKING UP
Press as described on the information page.
Join right shoulder seam using back stitch, or mattress stitch if preferred.

Collar
With RS facing and using 8mm (US 11) needles, pick up and knit 4 sts down left side of neck, patt 10 [10: 10: 12: 12] sts from front, pick up and knit 4 sts up right side of neck, then patt 14 [14: 14: 16: 16] sts from back. 32 [32: 32: 36: 36] sts.
Change to 10mm (US 15) needles.
Cont in patt as set by back neck sts until collar meas 21 cm.
Cast off in patt.
See information page for finishing instructions, setting in sleeves using the shallow set-in method and leaving collar seam open.

No. 8

VENUS

YARN

	XS	S	M	L	XL	
To fit bust	81	86	91	97	102	cm
	32	34	36	38	40	in

Rowan Spray and Big Wool

A Spray Mellow 002						
	5	5	5	6	6	x100gm
B Big Ice Blue 021						
	2	2	2	2	2	x100gm

NEEDLES
1 pair 8mm (no 0) (US 11) needles
1 pair 10mm (no 000) (US 15) needles

BUTTONS – 26 x (00316) and 23 x (00315)

TENSION
9 sts and 11 rows to 10 cm measured over stocking stitch using 10mm (US 15) needles.

BACK
Using 8mm (US 11) needles and yarn A cast on 41 [43: 45: 49: 51] sts.
Row 1 (RS): K1, *P1, K1, rep from * to end.
Row 2: P1, *K1, P1, rep from * to end.
These 2 rows form rib.
Work in rib for a further 3 rows, ending with **WS** facing for next row.
Change to 10mm (US 15) needles.
Beg with a **P** row, work in st st for 3 rows, ending with RS facing for next row.
Next row (dec) (RS): K1, sl 1, K1, psso, K to last 3 sts, K2tog, K1.
Working all side seam decreases as set by last row, dec 1 st at each end of 6th and foll 4th row. 35 [37: 39: 43: 45] sts.
Work 3 rows, ending with RS facing for next row.
Next row (inc) (RS): K1, M1, K to last st, M1, K1.
Working all side seam increases as set by last row, inc 1 st at each end of 6th and foll 4th row.
41 [43: 45: 49: 51] sts.
Break off yarn A and join in yarn B.
Working next 12 rows using yarn B and then completing back using yarn A, cont as folls:
Cont straight until back meas 35 [36: 36: 37: 37] cm, ending with RS facing for next row.
Shape armholes
Dec 1 st at each end of next 4 rows.
33 [35: 37: 41: 43] sts.
Cont straight until armhole meas 20 [20: 21: 21: 22] cm, ending with RS facing for next row.
Shape shoulders
Cast off 8 [9: 10: 11: 12] sts at beg of next 2 rows.
Break yarn and leave rem 17 [17: 17: 19: 19] sts on a holder.

FRONT
Work as given for back until 6 rows less have been worked than on back to beg of shoulder shaping, ending with RS facing for next row.
Shape neck
Next row (RS): K11 [12: 13: 14: 15] and turn, leaving rem sts on a holder.
Work each side of neck separately.
Dec 1 st at neck edge of next 3 rows. 8 [9: 10: 11: 12] sts.

Work 2 rows, ending with RS facing for next row.

Shape shoulder

Cast off.

With RS facing, slip centre 11 [11: 11: 13: 13] sts onto a holder, rejoin yarn to rem sts, K to end.

Complete to match first side, reversing shapings.

SLEEVES

Using 8mm (US 11) needles and yarn B cast on 19 [19: 21: 21: 23] sts.

Work in rib as given for back for 4 rows, ending with RS facing for next row.

Change to 10mm (US 15) needles.

Beg with a K row, work in st st, shaping sides by inc 1 st at each end of next and foll 4th [4th: 6th: 6th: 6th] row, then on foll 6th [6th: -: -: -] row.

25 [25: 25: 25: 27] sts.

Work 1 [1: 5: 5: 5] rows, ending with RS facing for next row.

Break off yarn B and join in yarn A.

Cont in st st, inc 1 st at each end of 5th [5th: next: next: next] and every foll 6th row until there are 35 [35: 37: 37: 39] sts.

Cont straight until sleeve meas 45 [45: 46: 46: 46] cm, ending with RS facing for next row.

Shape top

Dec 1 st at each end of next 4 rows, ending with RS facing for next row.

Cast off rem 27 [27: 29: 29: 31] sts.

MAKING UP

Press as described on the information page.

Join right shoulder seam using back stitch, or mattress stitch if preferred.

Neckband

With RS facing, using 8mm (US 11) needles and yarn A, pick up and knit 5 sts down left side of neck, K11 [11: 11: 13: 13] sts from front, pick up and knit 4 sts up right side of neck, then K17 [17: 17: 19: 19] sts from back.

37 [37: 37: 41: 41] sts.

Beg with row 2, work in rib as given for back for 7 cm.

Cast off in rib.

See information page for finishing instructions, setting in sleeves using the shallow set-in method.

Using photo as a guide and chain st, embroider circles onto front – use yarn A where circle falls on knitted section in yarn B and vice versa. Attach buttons as in photograph, making a third circle of buttons only near lower edge.

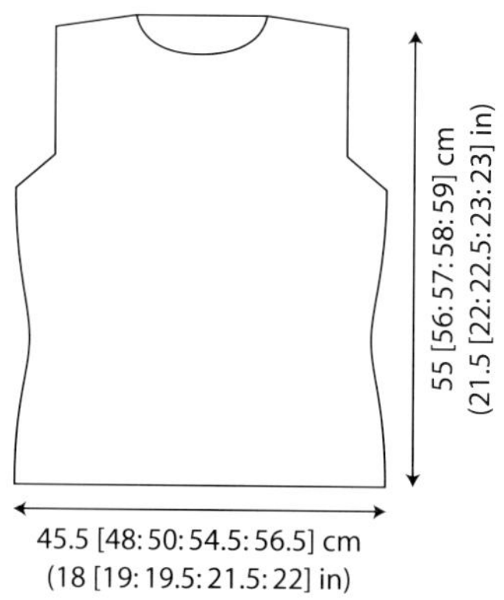

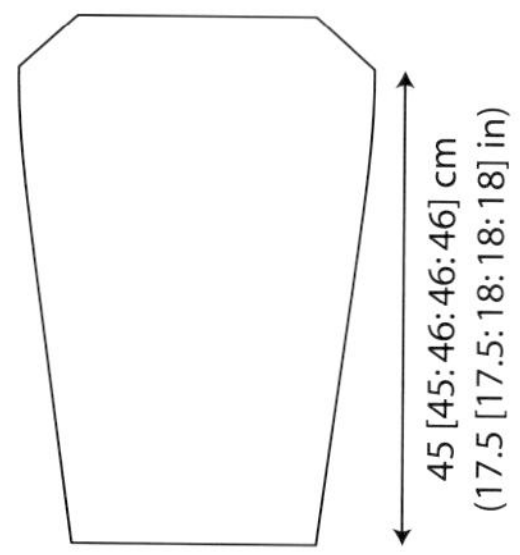

No. 9 & 10

SKULK & MOODY

YARN

Two colour hat

Rowan Spray and Big Wool

A Spray Mellow 002
1 x 100gm

B Big Camouflage 023
1 x 100gm

One colour hat

Rowan Spray
1 x 100gm
(photographed in Languid 003)

NEEDLES

1 pair 8mm (no 0) (US 11) needles
1 pair 10mm (no 000) (US 15) needles

TENSION

9 sts and 11 rows to 10 cm measured over stocking stitch using 10mm (US 15) needles.

One colour hat

Work as given for two colour hat (below) but using same colour throughout.

Two colour hat

Using 8mm (US 11) needles and yarn A cast on 45 sts.

Row 1 (RS): K1, *P1, K1, rep from * to end.

Row 2: P1, *K1, P1, rep from * to end.

These 2 rows form rib.

Work in rib for a further 2 rows, ending with RS facing for next row.

Change to 10mm (US 15) needles.

Beg with a K row, work in st st for 2 rows, ending with RS facing for next row.

Beg and ending rows as indicated and using the **fairisle** technique as described on the information page, cont in patt from chart, which is worked entirely in st st beg with a K row, until chart row 8 has been completed, ending with RS facing for next row.

Shape crown

Row 1 (RS): (K9, K2tog) 4 times, K1. 41 sts.

Row 2 and every foll alt row: Purl.

Row 3: (K7, K3tog) 4 times, K1. 33 sts.

Row 5: (K5, K3tog) 4 times, K1. 25 sts.

Row 7: (K3, K3tog) 4 times, K1. 17 sts.

Row 8: P1, (P2tog) 8 times.

Break yarn and thread through rem 9 sts. Pull up tight and fasten off securely.

MAKING UP

Press as described on the information page.

Join back seam.

Key □ A ■ B

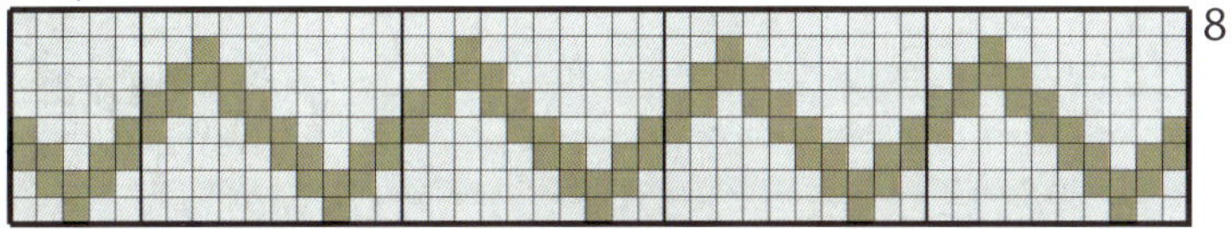

No. 11

SASSY

YARN

	XS-S	M	L-XL	
To fit bust	81-86	91	97-102	cm
	32-34	36	38-40	in

Rowan Spray and Big Wool

A Spray	Calm00007			
	7	8	9	x100gm
B Big Wool	Latte 018			
	1	1	1	x100gm

NEEDLES
1 pair 8mm (no 0) (US 11) needles
1 pair 10mm (no 000) (US 15) needles
8mm (no 0) (US 11) circular needle

BUTTONS – 6 x 00354

TENSION
9 sts and 11 rows to 10 cm measured over stocking stitch using 10mm (US 15) needles.

BACK
Using 8mm (US 11) needles and yarn A cast on 45 [47: 49] sts.
Row 1 (RS): K1, *P1, K1, rep from * to end.
Row 2: P1, *K1, P1, rep from * to end.
These 2 rows form rib.
Work in rib for a further 2 rows, ending with RS facing for next row.
Change to 10mm (US 15) needles.
Beg with a K row, work in st st until back meas 35 [36: 37] cm, ending with RS facing for next row.
Dec 1 st at each end of next and every foll 4th row to 27 [31: 33] sts, then on foll 5 [7: 7] alt rows.
17 [17: 19] sts.**
Work 1 row, ending with RS facing for next row.
Cast off.

FRONT
Work as given for back to **, ending with **WS** facing for next row.
Cast off knitwise (on **WS**).

SIDE PANELS (make 2)
Using 8mm (US 11) needles and yarn A cast on 23 [25: 27] sts.
Work in rib as given for back for 4 rows, ending with RS facing for next row.
Change to 10mm (US 15) needles.
Beg with a K row, work in st st until side panel meas 35 [36: 37] cm, ending with RS facing for next row.
Dec 1 st at each end of next and every foll 8th [6th: 6th] row to 15 [9: 15] sts, then on every foll 6th [-: 4th] row until 9 [-: 9] sts rem.
Work 1 row, ending with RS facing for next row.
Cast off.

MAKING UP
Press as described on the information page.
Join side panels to back using back stitch, or mattress stitch if preferred.
Front edgings (both alike)
With RS facing, using 8mm (US 11) needles and yarn B, pick up and knit 79 [80: 81] sts along row-end edge of front, between cast-on and cast-off edges.
Cast off knitwise (on **WS**).
Join front to side panels so that front edgings show and leaving 23 cm openings (for hands) approx 15 cm up from cast-on edge.
Place markers on front neck (cast-off) edge, 6 [6: 7] cm in from panel seams.
Collar
With RS facing, using 8mm (US 11) circular needle and yarn A, beg and ending at markers, pick up and knit 6 [6: 7] sts from

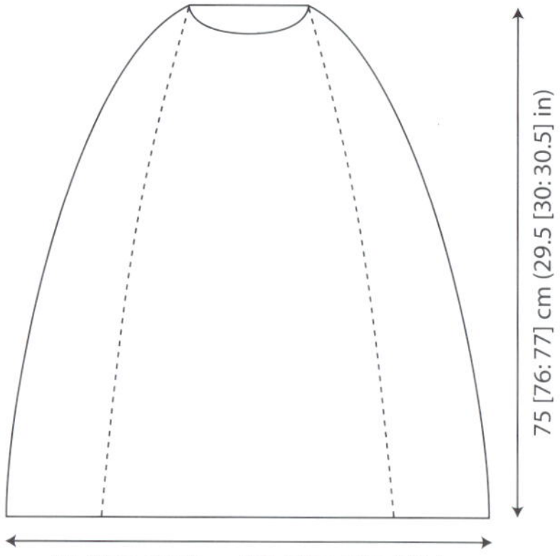

right side of front neck, 8 sts from side panel, 17 [17: 19] sts from back, 8 sts from side panel, then 6 [6: 7] sts from left side of front neck to marker.
45 [45: 49] sts.

Beg with row 1, work in rib as given for back for 6 rows.
Row 7 (RS of collar, WS of body): K1, *inc in next st, K1, rep from * to end.
67 [67: 73] sts.

Row 8: P1, *K2, P1, rep from * to end.
Row 9: K1, *P2, K1, rep from * to end.
Rep last 2 rows until collar meas 14 cm from pick-up row.
Cast off in rib.

See information page for finishing instructions.
Using photograph as a guide, sew on buttons, then embroider chain st mock buttonholes around buttons using B.

No. 12

BEAT

YARN

	XS	S	M	L	XL	
To fit bust	81	86	91	97	102	cm
	32	34	36	38	40	in

Rowan Spray

6	6	7	7	7	x100gm

(photographed in Landscape 001)

NEEDLES
1 pair 8mm (no 0) (US 11) needles
1 pair 10mm (no 000) (US 15) needles

TENSION
9 sts and 11 rows to 10 cm measured over stocking stitch using 10mm (US 15) needles.

BACK
Using 8mm (US 11) needles cast on 42 [46: 46: 50: 54] sts.
Row 1 (RS): K2, *P2, K2, rep from * to end.
Row 2: P2, *K2, P2, rep from * to end.
These 2 rows form rib.
Work in rib for a further 2 rows, dec 0 [1: 0: 0: 1] st at each end of last row and ending with RS facing for next row. 42 [44: 46: 50: 52] sts.
Change to 10mm (US 15) needles.
Row 1 (RS): K4 [5: 6: 8: 9], wrap next st (by slipping next st onto right needle, bringing yarn to RS of work between needles and then slipping same st back onto left needle – when working back across wrapped sts, work the wrapped st and the loop tog), turn.
Row 2 and every foll alt row: Purl.
Row 3: K11 [12: 13: 15: 16], wrap next st and turn.
Row 5: K18 [19: 20: 22: 23], wrap next st and turn.
Row 7: K25 [26: 27: 29: 30], wrap next st and turn.
Row 9: K32 [33: 34: 36: 37], wrap next st and turn.
Row 11: K39 [40: 41: 43: 44], wrap next st and turn.
Row 12: Purl.
Beg with a K row, work in st st across all sts until back meas 36 [37: 37: 38: 38] cm **at longer edge**, ending with RS facing for next row.
Shape armholes
Dec 1 st at each end of next 4 rows.
34 [36: 38: 42: 44] sts.
Cont straight until armhole meas 20 [20: 21: 21: 22] cm, ending with RS facing for next row.
Shape shoulders
Cast off, placing markers either side of centre 16 [16: 16: 18: 18] sts to denote back neck.

FRONT
Using 8mm (US 11) needles cast on 42 [46: 46: 50: 54] sts.

Work in rib as given for back for 4 rows, dec 0 [1: 0: 0: 1] st at each end of last row and ending with RS facing for next row.
42 [44: 46: 50: 52] sts.
Change to 10mm (US 15) needles.
Row 1 (RS): K38 [39: 40: 42: 43], wrap next st and turn.
Row 2 and every foll alt row: Purl.
Row 3: K31 [32: 33: 35: 36], wrap next st and turn.
Row 5: K24 [25: 26: 28: 29], wrap next st and turn.
Row 7: K17 [18: 19: 21: 22], wrap next st and turn.
Row 9: K10 [11: 12: 14: 15], wrap next st and turn.
Row 11: K3 [4: 5: 7: 8], wrap next st and turn.
Row 12: Purl.
Beg with a K row, work in st st across all sts until front matches back to beg of armhole shaping, ending with RS facing for next row.

Shape armholes

Dec 1 st at each end of next 4 rows. 34 [36: 38: 42: 44] sts.
Cont straight until 8 rows less have been worked than on back to beg of shoulder shaping, ending with RS facing for next row.

Shape neck

Next row (RS): K12 [13: 14: 15: 16] and turn, leaving rem sts on a holder.
Work each side of neck separately.
Dec 1 st at neck edge of next 3 rows. 9 [10: 11: 12: 13] sts.
Work 4 rows, ending with RS facing for next row.

Shape shoulder

Cast off.
With RS facing, rejoin yarn to rem sts, cast off centre 10 [10: 10: 12: 12] sts, K to end.
Complete to match first side, reversing shapings.

SLEEVES

Using 8mm (US 11) needles cast on 18 [18: 20: 20: 22] sts.
Row 1 (RS): P0 [0: 1: 1: 0], K2, *P2, K2, rep from * to last 0 [0: 1: 1: 0] st, P0 [0: 1: 1: 0].
Row 2: K0 [0: 1: 1: 0], P2, *K2, P2, rep from * to last 0 [0: 1: 1: 0] st, K0 [0: 1: 1: 0].
These 2 rows form rib.
Work in rib for a further 10 rows, ending with RS facing for next row.
Change to 10mm (US 15) needles.
Beg with a K row, work in st st, shaping sides by inc 1 st at each end of next and every foll 4th row to 36 [36: 36: 36: 38] sts, then on foll – [-: 6th: 6th: 6th] row. 36 [36: 38: 38: 40] sts.
Cont straight until sleeve meas 45 [45: 46: 46: 46] cm, ending with RS facing for next row.

Shape top

Dec 1 st at each end of next 4 rows, ending with RS facing for next row.
Cast off rem 28 [28: 30: 30: 32] sts.

MAKING UP

Press as described on the information page.
Join right shoulder seam using back stitch, or mattress stitch if preferred.

Neckband

With RS facing and using 8mm (US 11) needles, pick up and knit 8 sts down left side of neck, 10 [10: 10: 12: 12] sts from front, 8 sts up right side of neck, then 16 [16: 16: 18: 18] sts from back. 42 [42: 42: 46: 46] sts.
Beg with row 2, work in rib as given for back for 11 rows, ending with RS facing for next row.
Cast off in rib.
See information page for finishing instructions, setting in sleeves using the shallow set-in method.

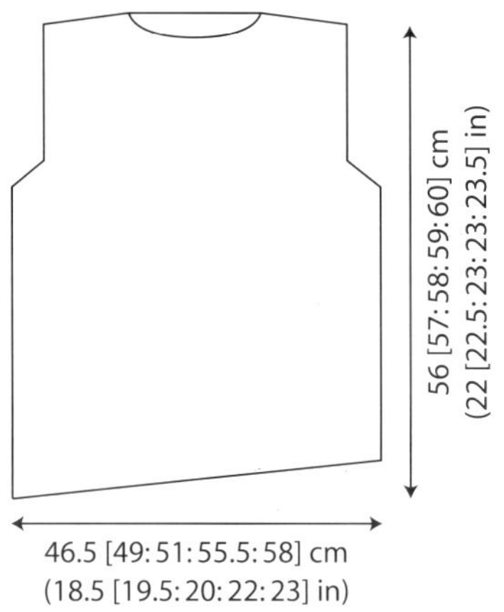

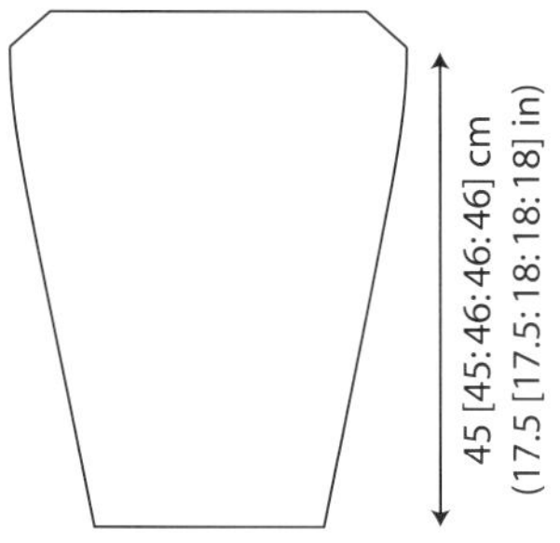

No. 13

CLASH

YARN

	XS	S	M	L	XL	
To fit bust	81	86	91	97	102	cm
	32	34	36	38	40	in

Longer version

Rowan Spray

7	7	8	8	9	x100gm

(photographed in Landscape 001)

Shorter version

Rowan Spray and Big Wool

A SpraySeascape006

6	6	6	7	7	x100gm

B Big WoolBlue Velvet 026

1	1	1	1	1	x100gm

NEEDLES

1 pair 8mm (no 0) (US 11) needles
1 pair 10mm (no 000) (US 15) needles
8mm (no 0) (US 11) circular needle

BUTTONS – 3 x 00343 for longer version, or 4 x 00359 & 00373 for shorter version

TENSION

9 sts and 11 rows to 10 cm measured over stocking stitch using 10mm (US 15) needles.

Longer version

BACK
Using 8mm (US 11) needles cast on 41 [43: 45: 49: 51] sts.
Row 1 (RS): K1, *P1, K1, rep from * to end.
Row 2: P1, *K1, P1, rep from * to end.
These 2 rows form rib.
Work in rib for a further 3 rows, ending with **WS** facing for next row.
Change to 10mm (US 15) needles.
Beg with a **P** row, work in st st for 21 rows, ending with RS facing for next row.
Next row (RS): K2, sl 1, K1, psso, K to last 4 sts, K2tog, K2.
Working all side seam decreases as set by last row, dec 1 st at each end of 2nd and foll 4th row.
35 [37: 39: 43: 45] sts.
Cont straight until back meas 35 [36: 36: 37: 37] cm, ending with RS facing for next row.
****Next row (RS):** K2, M1, K to last 2 sts, M1, K2.
Working all side seam increases as set by last row, inc 1 st at each end of 4th and foll 4th row.
41 [43: 45: 49: 51] sts.
Work 11 rows, ending with RS facing for next row.
Shape armholes
Cast off 3 sts at beg of next 2 rows.
35 [37: 39: 43: 45] sts.
Dec 1 st at each end of next 1 [1: 1: 3: 3] rows, then on foll 2 [2: 3: 2: 3] alt rows.
29 [31: 31: 33: 33] sts.
Cont straight until armhole meas 20 [20: 21: 21: 22] cm, ending with RS facing for next row.
Shape shoulders
Cast off 7 [8: 8: 8: 8] sts at beg of next 2 rows.
Break yarn and leave rem 15 [15: 15: 17: 17] sts on a holder.

LEFT FRONT
Using 8mm (US 11) needles cast on 20 [20: 22: 24: 24] sts.
Row 1 (RS): *K1, P1, rep from * to end.
Row 2: As row 1.
These 2 rows form rib.
Work in rib for a further 3 rows, dec 1 [0: 1: 1: 0] st at beg of last row and ending with **WS** facing for next row.
19 [20: 21: 23: 24] sts.
Change to 10mm (US 15) needles.
Beg with a **P** row, work in st st for 21 rows, ending with RS facing for next row.
Next row (RS): K2, sl 1, K1, psso, K to end.
Working all side seam decreases as set by last row, dec 1 st at beg of 2nd and foll 4th row.
16 [17: 18: 20: 21] sts.
Cont straight until left front meas 35 [36: 36: 37: 37] cm, ending with RS facing for next row.
*****Next row (RS):** K2, M1, K to end.
Working all side seam increases as set by last row, inc 1 st at beg of 4th and foll 4th row.
19 [20: 21: 23: 24] sts.
Work 5 rows, ending with RS facing for next row.
Shape front slope
Dec 1 st at end of next and foll 4th row.
17 [18: 19: 21: 22] sts.
Work 1 row, ending with RS facing for next row.

Shape armhole
Cast off 3 sts at beg of next row.
14 [15: 16: 18: 19] sts.
Work 1 row.
Dec 1 st at armhole edge of next 1 [1: 1: 3: 3] rows, then on foll 2 [2: 3: 2: 3] alt rows **and at same time** dec 1 st at front slope edge of next and every foll 4th row.
9 [10: 10: 11: 10] sts.
Dec 1 st at front slope edge **only** of 4th [4th: 4th: 2nd: 4th] and every foll 6th [6th: 6th: 4th: 4th] row until 7 [8: 8: 8: 8] sts rem.
Cont straight until left front matches back to beg of shoulder shaping, ending with RS facing for next row.
Shape shoulder
Cast off.

RIGHT FRONT
Using 8mm (US 11) needles cast on 20 [20: 22: 24: 24] sts.
Row 1 (RS): *P1, K1, rep from * to end.
Row 2: As row 1.
These 2 rows form rib.
Work in rib for a further 3 rows, dec 1 [0: 1: 1: 0] st at end of last row and ending with **WS** facing for next row.
19 [20: 21: 23: 24] sts.
Change to 10mm (US 15) needles.
Beg with a **P** row, work in st st for 21 rows, ending with RS facing for next row.
Next row (RS): K to last 4 sts, K2tog, K2.
Working all side seam decreases as set by last row, dec 1 st at end of 2nd and foll 4th row.
16 [17: 18: 20: 21] sts.
Complete to match left front, reversing shapings, working an extra row before beg of armhole and shoulder shaping.

SLEEVES
Using 8mm (US 11) needles cast on 19 [19: 21: 21: 23] sts.
Work in rib as given for back for 4 rows, ending with RS facing for next row.
Change to 10mm (US 15) needles.
Beg with a K row, work in st st, shaping sides by inc 1 st at each end of 5th and every foll 6th row until there are 33 [33: 35: 35: 37] sts.
Cont straight until sleeve meas 45 [45: 46: 46: 46] cm, ending with RS facing for next row.
Shape top
Cast off 3 sts at beg of next 2 rows.
27 [27: 29: 29: 31] sts.
Dec 1 st at each end of next 3 rows, then on foll alt row, then on foll 4th row.
17 [17: 19: 19: 21] sts.
Work 1 row, ending with RS facing for next row.
Dec 1 st at each end of next and every foll alt row until 13 sts rem, then on foll row, ending with RS facing for next row.
Cast off rem 11 sts.

MAKING UP
Press as described on the information page.
Join shoulder seams using back stitch, or mattress stitch if preferred.
Front band
With RS facing and using 8mm (US 11) circular needle, beg and ending at cast-on edges, pick up and knit 48 [49: 49: 50: 50] sts up right front opening edge to beg of front slope shaping, 24 [24: 25: 25: 26] sts up right front slope to shoulder, K15 [15: 15: 17: 17] sts from back, pick up and knit 24 [24: 25: 25: 26] sts down left front slope to beg of front slope shaping, then 48 [49: 49: 50: 50] sts down left front opening edge.
159 [161: 163: 167: 169] sts.
Beg with row 2, work in rib as given for back for 1 row, ending with RS facing for next row.
Row 2 (RS): Rib 28 [29: 29: 30: 30], *yrn, work 2 tog (to make a buttonhole), rib 6, rep from * once more, yrn, work 2 tog (to make 3rd buttonhole), rib to end.
Work in rib for 1 row more, ending with RS facing for next row.
Cast off in rib.
See information page for finishing instructions, setting in sleeves using the set-in method.

Shorter version

BACK
Using 8mm (US 11) needles and yarn A cast on 41 [43: 45: 49: 51] sts.
Row 1 (RS): K1, *P1, K1, rep from * to end.
Row 2: P1, *K1, P1, rep from * to end.
These 2 rows form rib.
Work in rib for a further 3 rows, ending with **WS** facing for next row.
Change to 10mm (US 15) needles.
Beg with a **P** row, work in st st for 1 row, ending with RS facing for next row.
Next row (RS): K2, sl 1, K1, psso, K to last 4 sts, K2tog, K2.
Working all side seam decreases as set by last row, dec 1 st at each end of 2nd and foll 4th row.
35 [37: 39: 43: 45] sts.
Cont straight until back meas 17 [18: 18: 19: 19] cm, ending with RS facing for next row.
Complete as given for back of longer version from **.

LEFT FRONT
Using 8mm (US 11) needles and yarn A cast on 20 [20: 22: 24: 24] sts.
Row 1 (RS): *K1, P1, rep from * to end.
Row 2: As row 1.
These 2 rows form rib.
Work in rib for a further 3 rows, dec 1 [0: 1: 1: 0] st at beg of last row and ending with **WS** facing for next row. 19 [20: 21: 23: 24] sts.
Change to 10mm (US 15) needles.
Beg with a **P** row, work in st st for 1 row, ending with RS facing for next row.
Next row (RS): K2, sl 1, K1, psso, K to end.
Working all side seam decreases as set by last row, dec 1 st at beg of 2nd and foll 4th row.
16 [17: 18: 20: 21] sts.
Cont straight until left front meas 17 [18: 18: 19: 19] cm, ending with RS facing for next row.
Complete as given for left front of longer version from ***.

RIGHT FRONT
Using 8mm (US 11) needles and yarn A cast on 20 [20: 22: 24: 24] sts.
Row 1 (RS): *P1, K1, rep from * to end.
Row 2: As row 1.
These 2 rows form rib.
Work in rib for a further 3 rows, dec 1 [0: 1: 1: 0] st at end of last row and ending with **WS** facing for next row.
19 [20: 21: 23: 24] sts.
Change to 10mm (US 15) needles.
Beg with a **P** row, work in st st for 1 row, ending with RS facing for next row.
Next row (RS): K to last 4 sts, K2tog, K2.
Working all side seam decreases as

set by last row, dec 1 st at end of 2nd and foll 4th row.
16 [17: 18: 20: 21] sts.
Complete to match left front, reversing shapings, working an extra row before beg of armhole and shoulder shaping.

SLEEVES
Using yarn A, work as given for sleeves of longer version.

MAKING UP
Press as described on the information page.
Join shoulder seams using back stitch, or mattress stitch if preferred.
Front band
With RS facing, using 8mm (US 11) circular needle and yarn B, beg and ending at cast-on edges, pick up and knit 28 [29: 29: 30: 30] sts up right front opening edge to beg of front slope shaping, 24 [24: 25: 25: 26] sts up right front slope to shoulder, K15 [15: 15: 17: 17] sts from back, pick up and knit 24 [24: 25: 25: 26] sts down left front slope to beg of front slope shaping, then 28 [29: 29: 30: 30] sts down left front opening edge.
119 [121: 123: 127: 129] sts.
Beg with row 2, work in rib as given for back for 1 row, ending with RS facing for next row.
Row 2 (RS): Rib 2 [3: 3: 3: 3], *yrn, work 2 tog (to make a buttonhole), rib 6, rep from * twice more, yrn, work 2 tog (to make 4th buttonhole), rib to end.
Work in rib for 1 row more, ending with RS facing for next row.
Cast off in rib.
See information page for finishing instructions, setting in sleeves using the set-in method.

When attaching buttons, place a small button on top of a large button and attach both at same time to creat decorative button trim as in photograph.

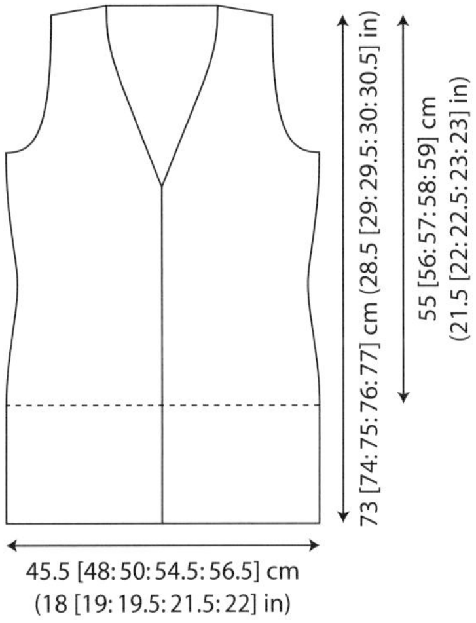

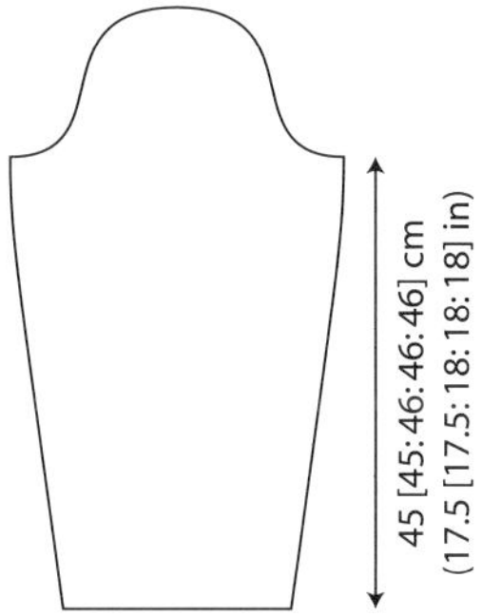

No. 14

QUIRK

YARN

	XS	S	M	L	XL	
To fit bust	81	86	91	97	102	cm
	32	34	36	38	40	in
Rowan Spray						
	6	7	7	8	8	x100gm

(photographed in Languid 00003)

NEEDLES
1 pair 8mm (no 0) (US 11) needles
1 pair 10mm (no 000) (US 15) needles

BUTTONS – 6 x 00357 and 6 x 00375

TENSION
9 sts and 11 rows to 10 cm measured over stocking stitch using 10mm (US 15) needles.

BACK
Using 8mm (US 11) needles cast on 41 [43: 45: 49: 51] sts.
Row 1 (RS): K1, *P1, K1, rep from * to end.
Row 2: P1, *K1, P1, rep from * to end.
These 2 rows form rib.
Work in rib for a further 2 rows, ending with RS facing for next row.
Change to 10mm (US 15) needles.
Work in rib for a further 12 rows, ending with RS facing for next row.
Beg with a K row, work in st st until back meas 35 [36: 36: 37: 37] cm, ending with RS facing for next row.
Shape armholes
Cast off 2 sts at beg of next 2 rows.
37 [39: 41: 45: 47] sts.
Dec 1 st at each end of next 1 [1: 1: 3: 3] rows, then on foll 1 [1: 2: 1: 2] alt rows. 33 [35: 35: 37: 37] sts.
Cont straight until armhole meas 20 [20: 21: 21: 22] cm, ending with RS facing for next row.
Shape shoulders
Cast off 5 [6: 6: 6: 6] sts at beg of next 2 rows.
Break yarn and leave rem 23 [23: 23: 25: 25] sts on a holder.

LEFT FRONT
Using 8mm (US 11) needles cast on 14 [14: 16: 18: 18] sts.
Row 1 (RS): *K1, P1, rep from * to end.
Row 2: As row 1.
These 2 rows form rib.
Work in rib for a further 2 rows, ending with RS facing for next row.
Change to 10mm (US 15) needles.
Work in rib for a further 12 rows, dec 1 [0: 1: 1: 0] st at end of last row and ending with RS facing for next row.
13 [14: 15: 17: 18] sts.
Beg with a K row, work in st st until left front matches back to beg of armhole shaping, ending with RS facing for next row.
Shape armhole
Cast off 2 sts at beg of next row.
11 [12: 13: 15: 16] sts.
Work 1 row.
Dec 1 st at armhole edge of next 1 [1: 1: 3: 3] rows, then on foll 1 [1: 2: 1: 2] alt rows.
9 [10: 10: 11: 11] sts.
Cont straight until 7 rows less have been worked than on back to beg of shoulder shaping, ending with **WS** facing for next row.
Shape neck
Cast off 2 [2: 2: 3: 3] sts at beg of next row.
7 [8: 8: 8: 8] sts.
Dec 1 st at neck edge of next and foll alt row.
5 [6: 6: 6: 6] sts.
Work 3 rows, ending with RS facing for next row.
Shape shoulder
Cast off.

RIGHT FRONT
Using 8mm (US 11) needles cast on 26 [26: 28: 30: 30] sts.
Row 1 (RS): *P1, K1, rep from * to end.
Row 2: As row 1.
These 2 rows form rib.
Work in rib for a further 2 rows, ending with RS facing for next row.
Change to 10mm (US 15) needles.
Work in rib for a further 12 rows, dec 1 [0: 1: 1: 0] st at beg of last row and ending with RS facing for next row.
25 [26: 27: 29: 30] sts.
Beg with a K row, work in st st until right front matches back to beg of armhole shaping, ending with **WS** facing for next row.
Shape armhole
Cast off 2 sts at beg of next row.

23 [24: 25: 27: 28] sts.
Dec 1 st at armhole edge of next 1 [1: 1: 3: 3] rows, then on foll 1 [1: 2: 1: 2] alt rows.
21 [22: 22: 23: 23] sts.
Cont straight until 8 rows less have been worked than on back to beg of shoulder shaping, ending with RS facing for next row.

Shape neck

Cast off 14 [14: 14: 15: 15] sts at beg of next row.
7 [8: 8: 8: 8] sts.
Dec 1 st at neck edge of next and foll alt row.
5 [6: 6: 6: 6] sts.
Work 5 rows, ending with **WS** facing for next row.

Shape shoulder

Cast off.

SLEEVES

Using 8mm (US 11) needles cast on 19 [19: 21: 21: 23] sts.
Work in rib as given for back for 4 rows, ending with RS facing for next row.
Change to 10mm (US 15) needles.
Cont in rib, inc 1 st at each end of 5th and foll 6th row.
23 [23: 25: 25: 27] sts.
Work a further 3 rows, ending with RS facing for next row.
Beg with a K row, work in st st, shaping sides by inc 1 st at each end of 3rd and every foll 6th row until there are 33 [33: 35: 35: 37] sts.
Cont straight until sleeve meas 45 [45: 46: 46: 46] cm, ending with RS facing for next row.

Shape top

Cast off 2 sts at beg of next 2 rows.
29 [29: 31: 31: 33] sts.
Dec 1 st at each end of next 3 rows, then on every foll alt row to 17 sts, then on foll 3 rows, ending with RS facing for next row.
Cast off rem 11 sts.

MAKING UP

Press as described on the information page.
Join shoulder seams using back stitch, or mattress stitch if preferred.

Neckband

With RS facing and using 8mm (US 11) needles, beg and ending at front opening edges, pick up and knit 19 [19: 19: 20: 20] sts up right side of neck, K23 [23: 23: 25: 25] sts from back, then pick up and knit 7 [7: 7: 8: 8] sts down left side of neck.
49 [49: 49: 53: 53] sts.
Beg with row 2, work in rib as given for back for 4 rows, ending with **WS** facing for next row.
Cast off in rib (on **WS**).

Button band

With RS facing and using 8mm (US 11) needles, beg at top of neckband, pick up and knit 51 [53: 53: 55: 55] sts down left front opening edge to cast-on edge.
Beg with row 2, work in rib as given for back for 4 rows, ending with **WS** facing for next row.
Cast off in rib (on **WS**).

Buttonhole band

With RS facing and using 8mm (US 11) needles, beg at cast-on edge, pick up and knit 51 [53: 53: 55: 55] sts up right front opening edge to top of neckband.
Beg with row 2, work in rib as given for back for 1 row, ending with RS facing for next row.
Row 2 (RS): Rib 2 [4: 4: 1: 1], *work 2 tog, yrn (to make a buttonhole), rib 7 [7: 7: 8: 8], rep from * to last 4 sts, work 2 tog, yrn (to make 6th buttonhole), rib 2.
Work in rib for a further 2 rows, ending with **WS** facing for next row.
Cast off in rib (on **WS**).

Pocket trim

Using 8mm (US 11) needles cast on 9 sts.
Beg with row 1, work in rib as given for back for 4 rows, ending with RS facing for next row.
Cast off in rib.
See information page for finishing instructions, setting in sleeves using the set-in method. Sew pocket trim onto right front as in photograph.
When attaching buttons, place a small button on top of a large button and attach both at same time to create decorative button trim as in photograph.

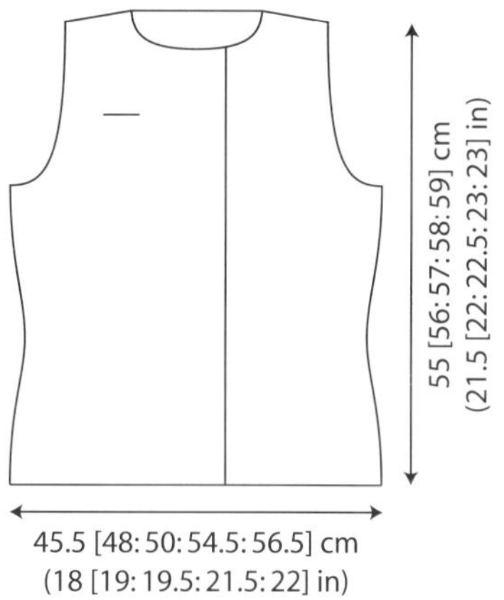

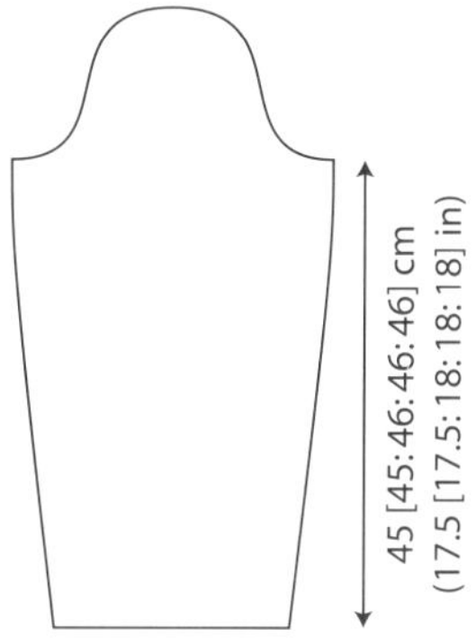

No. 15

RARE

YARN

Plain bag

Rowan Spray

5 x 100gm

(photographed in Sunset 004)

Bag with flap

Rowan Spray and Big Wool

A Spray Seascape 006

5 x 100gm

B Big Wool Blue Velvet 026

2 x 100gm

NEEDLES

1 pair 8mm (no 0) (US 11) needles

EXTRAS – 42 cm zip.
Plain bag: 4 x 00366 buckles.
Bag with flap: 1 x 00365 buckle.

FINISHED SIZE

Completed bag measures 45 cm (17½in) wide and 30 cm (12 in) deep.

TENSION

10 sts and 12½ rows to 10 cm measured over stocking stitch using 8mm (US 11) needles.

Plain bag

SIDES (make 2)
Using 8mm (US 11) needles cast on 45 sts.
Beg with a K row, work in st st for 30 cm, ending with RS facing for next row.
Cast off.

GUSSETS (make 2)
Using 8mm (US 11) needles cast on 19 sts.
Beg with a K row, work in st st for 38 cm, ending with RS facing for next row.
Next row (RS): Sl 1, K1, psso, K to last 2 sts, K2tog.
Working all decreases as set by last row, dec 1 st at each end of 4th and every foll 4th row to 11 sts, then on foll 4 alt rows, ending with **WS** facing for next row. 3 sts.
Next row (WS): P3tog and fasten off.

STRAP
Using 8mm (US 11) needles cast on 5 sts.
Row 1 (RS): (K1, P1) twice, K1.
Row 2: (P1, K1) twice, P1.
Rep these 2 rows until strap meas 258 cm, ending with RS facing for next row.
Cast off.

MAKING UP
Press as described on the information page.
Join cast-on edges of gussets. Positioning gusset seam at centre of cast-on edge of sides and matching gusset fasten-off points to cast-off edges, sew gussets to sides. Sew zip into upper (cast-off) opening edge. Thread buckles onto strap, then join ends of strap to form one long loop. Mark centre point of strap. Positioning centre point and strap seam centrally along gussets, approx 20 cm apart, sew strap to gussets and sides as in photograph, sliding buckles along strap so that they sit just below opening edge.
See information page for finishing instructions.

Bag with flap

SIDES, GUSSETS and STRAP
Using yarn A, work as given for plain bag.

FLAP
Using 8mm (US 11) needles and yarn B cast on 48 sts.
Row 1 (RS): K2, *P2, K1, rep from * to last st, K1.
Row 2: K1, *P1, K2, rep from * to last 2 sts, P1, K1.
Rep these 2 rows until flap meas 23 cm, ending with RS facing for next row.
Cast off in patt.

FLAP STRAP
Using 8mm (US 11) needles and yarn B cast on 5 sts.
Work as for strap until flap strap meas 30 cm, ending with RS facing for next row.
Cast off in patt.

MAKING UP
Press as described on the information page.

Join cast-on edges of gussets. Positioning gusset seam at centre of cast-on edge of sides and matching gusset fasten-off points to cast-off edges, sew gussets to sides. Sew zip into upper (cast-off) opening edge. Sew flap strap centrally onto flap, matching cast-off edges, then sew cast-off edge of flap to back of bag, just below opening edge. Attach buckle to front of bag to correspond with free end of flap strap. Mark centre point of strap. Positioning centre point and strap seam centrally along gussets, approx 20 cm apart, sew strap to gussets and sides as in photograph, leaving strap free over top of flap. See information page for finishing instructions.

No. 16

LUSTY

YARN

	XS	S	M	L	XL	
To fit bust	81	86	91	97	102	cm
	32	34	36	38	40	in

Rowan Spray

A Sensation 008						
	5	5	6	6	6	x100gm
B Sunset 004						
	3	3	3	4	4	x100gm

NEEDLES

1 pair 8mm (no 0) (US 11) needles
1 pair 10mm (no 000) (US 15) needles

TENSION

9 sts and 11 rows to 10 cm measured over stocking stitch using 10mm (US 15) needles.

BACK

Using 8mm (US 11) needles and yarn A cast on 53 [55: 57: 61: 63] sts.
Work in g st for 2 rows, ending with RS facing for next row.
Change to 10mm (US 15) needles.
Using the **intarsia** method as described on the information page, cont in patt as folls:
Counting in from both ends of last row, place markers after 18th st in from both ends of row, and on centre st.
Row 1 (RS): Using yarn A P to first marker, slip marker onto right needle, using yarn B K to marked centre st, sl marked st, using yarn A K1, P to third marker, slip marker to right needle, using yarn B K to end.
Row 2: Using yarn B P to first marker, slip marker onto right needle, using yarn A K to marked centre st, using yarn B P marked st, K1, P to third marker, slip marker onto right needle, using yarn A K to end.
Row 3: Using yarn A P to within 2 sts of first marker, P2tog tbl, slip marker onto right needle, using yarn B M1, K to marked centre st, sl marked st, using yarn A K1, P to third marker, M1, slip marker to right needle, using yarn B sl 1, K1, psso, K to end.
Rows 2 and 3 form patt.
Work in patt for a further 23 rows, dec 1 st at each end of 4th and every foll 4th row and ending with RS facing for next row.
43 [45: 47: 51: 53] sts.
Side markers are now 1 st in from ends of rows. Remove these markers and break off side edge balls of yarn.
Row 27 (RS): Using yarn B K2tog, patt to last 2 sts, using yarn A P2tog. 41 [43: 45: 49: 51] sts.
Keeping sts correct as now set, cont straight until back meas 49 [50: 51: 52: 53] cm, ending with RS facing for next row.
Shape shoulders
Cast off 11 [12: 13: 14: 15] sts at beg of next 2 rows.
Break yarns and leave rem 19 [19: 19: 21: 21] sts on a holder.

FRONT

Using 8mm (US 11) needles and yarn A cast on 53 [55: 57: 61: 63] sts.
Work in g st for 2 rows, ending with RS facing for next row.
Change to 10mm (US 15) needles.
Using the **intarsia** method as described on the information page, cont in patt as folls:
Counting in from both ends of last row, place markers after 18th st in from both ends of row, and on centre st.
Row 1 (RS): Using yarn B K to first marker, slip marker onto right needle, using yarn A P to within 1 st of marked centre st, K1, using yarn B sl marked st, K to third marker, slip marker to right needle, using yarn A P to end.
Row 2: Using yarn A K to first marker, slip marker onto right needle, using yarn B P to within 1 st of marked centre st, K1, P marked st, using yarn A K to third marker, slip marker onto right needle, using yarn B P to end.
Row 3: Using yarn B K to within 2 sts of first marker, K2tog, slip marker onto right needle, using yarn A M1, P to within 1 st of marked centre st, K1, using yarn B sl marked st, K to third marker, M1, slip marker to right needle, using yarn A P2tog tbl, P to end.
Rows 2 and 3 form patt.
Work in patt for a further 23 rows, dec 1 st at each end of 4th and every foll 4th row and ending with RS facing for next row.
43 [45: 47: 51: 53] sts.
Side markers are now 1 st in from ends of rows. Remove these markers and break off side edge balls of yarn.
Row 27 (RS): Using yarn A P2tog, patt to last 2 sts, using yarn B K2tog. 41 [43: 45: 49: 51] sts.
Keeping sts correct as now set, cont straight until 6 rows less have been worked than on back to beg of shoulder shaping, ending with RS facing for next row.
Shape neck
Next row (RS): Patt 15 [16: 17: 18: 19] sts and turn, leaving rem sts on a holder.
Work each side of neck separately.
Dec 1 st at neck edge of next 4 rows.
11 [12: 13: 14: 15] sts.
Work 1 row, ending with RS facing for next row.
Shape shoulder
Cast off.
With RS facing, rejoin yarns to rem sts, cast off centre 11 [11: 11: 13: 13] sts, patt to end.
Complete to match first side, reversing shapings.

SLEEVES

Using 10mm (US 15) needles and yarn A cast on 27 [27: 29: 29: 31] sts.
Row 1 (RS): K1, *P1, K1, rep from * to end.
Row 2: P1, *K1, P1, rep from * to end.
Row 3: As row 1.
Beg with a **P** row, work in st st, shaping sides by inc 1 st at each end of 4th and every foll 10th [10th: 12th: 12th: 12th] row until there are 35 [35: 37: 37: 39] sts.
Cont straight until sleeve meas 46 [46: 47: 47: 47] cm, ending with RS facing for next row.
Cast off.

MAKING UP

Press as described on the information page.
Join right shoulder seam using back stitch, or mattress stitch if preferred.
Neckband
With RS facing, using 10mm (US 15) needles and yarn A, pick up and knit 8 sts down left side of neck, 11 [11: 11: 13: 13] sts from front, and 8 sts up right side of neck, then K19 [19: 19: 21: 21] sts from back.
46 [46: 46: 50: 50] sts.
Row 1 (WS): P2, *K2, P2, rep from * to end.
Row 2: K2, *P2, K2, rep from * to end.
These 2 rows form rib.
Cont in rib until neckband meas 10 cm.
Cast off in rib.
See information page for finishing instructions, setting in sleeves using the straight cast-off method.

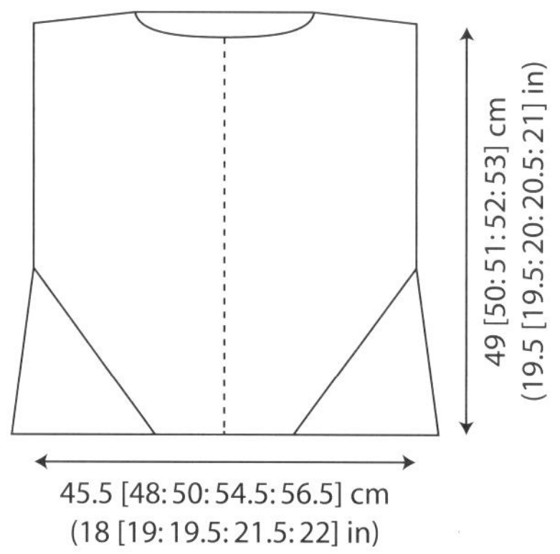

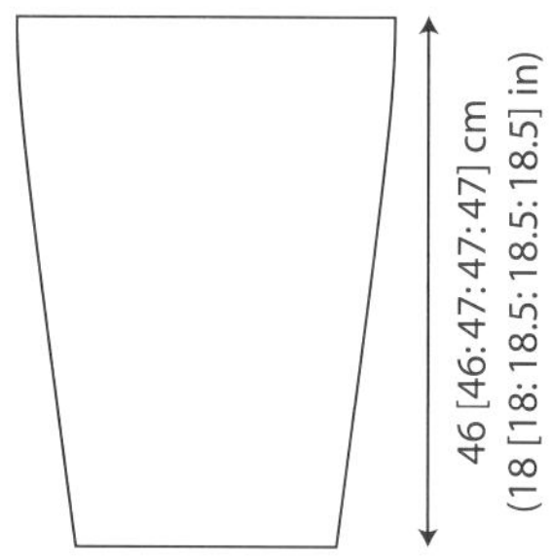

STOCKIST INFORMATION

ROWAN OVERSEAS DISTRIBUTORS

AUSTRALIA:
Australian Country Spinners
314 Albert Street
Brunswick
Victoria 3056
Tel: (03) 9380 3888
Email: sales@auspinners.com.au

BELGIUM:
Pavan
Meerlaanstraat 73
B9860 Balegem (Oosterzele)
Tel: (32) 9 221 8594
Email: pavan@pandora.be

CANADA:
Diamond Yarn
9697 St Laurent, Montreal
Quebec, H3L 2N1
Tel: (514) 388 6188

Diamond Yarn (Toronto),
155 Martin Ross, Unit 3
Toronto
Ontario, M3J 2L9
Tel: (416) 736 6111
Email: diamond@diamondyarn.com
www.diamondyarns.com

DENMARK
Individual stockists please contact Rowan for details

FRANCE:
Elle Tricot
8 Rue du Coq
67000 Strasbourg
Tel: (33) 3 88 23 03 13
Email: elletricot@agat.net
www.elletricote.com

GERMANY:
Wolle & Design
Wolfshovener Strasse 76
52428 Julich-Stetternich
Tel: (49) 2461 54735
Email: Info@wolleunddesign.de
www.wolleunddesign.de

Coats GMbH
Eduardstrasse 44
D-73084 Salach
Tel: (49) 7162 / 14-346
www.coatsgmbh.de

HOLLAND:
de Afstap
Oude Leliestraat 12
1015 AW Amsterdam
Tel: (31) 20 6231445

HONG KONG:
East Unity Co Ltd
Unit B2, 7/F Block B
Kailey Industrial Centre
12 Fung Yip Street, Chai Wan
Tel: (852) 2869 7110
Fax: (852) 2537 6952
Email: eastuni@netvigator.com

ICELAND:
Storkurinn
Laugavegi 59
101 Reykjavik
Tel: (354) 551 8258
Fax: (354) 562 8252
Email: malin@mmedia.is

ITALY:
D.L. srl
Via Piave, 24 – 26, 20016 Pero
Milan
Tel: (39) 02 339 10 180.

FINLAND:
Oy Nordia Produkter Ab
Mikkolantie 1
00640 Helsinki
Tel: (358) 9 777 4272
Email: info@nordiaprodukter.fi

JAPAN:
Puppy Co Ltd
T151-0051
3-16-5 Sendagaya
Shibuyaku, Tokyo
Tel: (81) 3 3490 2827
Email: info@rowan-jaeger.com

KOREA:
Coats Korea Co Ltd
5F Kuckdong B/D
935-40 Bangbae- Dong
Seocho-Gu, Seoul
Tel: (82) 2 521 6262
Fax: (82) 2 521 5181

NEW ZEALAND
Individual stockists please contact Rowan for details

NORWAY:
Coats Norge A/S
Postboks 63, 2801 Gjovik
Tel: (47) 61 18 34 00
Fax: (47) 61 18 34 20

SINGAPORE:
Golden Dragon Store
101 Upper Cross Street #02-51
People's Park Centre
Singapore 058357
Tel: (65) 6 5358454
Email: gdscraft@hotmail.com

SOUTH AFRICA:
Arthur Bales PTY
PO Box 44644
Linden 2104
Tel: (27) 11 888 2401

SPAIN:
Oyambre
Pau Claris 145, 80009 Barcelona
Tel: (34) 670 011957
Email: comercial@oyambreonline.com

SWEDEN:
Wincent
Norrtullsgatan 65, 113 45 Stockholm
Tel: (46) 8 33 70 60
Fax: (46) 8 33 70 68
Email: wincent@chello.se
www.wincentyarn.com

TAIWAN :
Laiter Wool Knitting Co Ltd
10-1 313 Lane, Sec 3
Chung Ching North Road
Taipei
Tel: (886) 2 2596 0269

Long T eh Trading Co Ltd
3F No. 19-2
Kung Yuan Road, Taichung
Tel: (886) 4 2225 6698

Green Leave Thread Company
No 181
Sec 4 Chung Ching North Road
Taipei
Fax: (886) 2 8221 2919

U.S.A.:
Westminster Fibers Inc
4 Townsend West
Suite 8, Nashua
New Hampshire 03063
Tel: (1 603) 886 5041 / 5043
Email: rowan@westminsterfibers.com

U.K.:
Rowan Yarns
Green Lane Mill, Holmfirth
West Yorkshire, HD9 2DX.
Tel : 01484 681881
Email: bigitup@knitrowan.com.
www.knitrowan.com

For all other countries:
please contact Rowan for stockist details.

For details of U.K. stockists or any other information concerning this brochure please contact:
Rowan Yarns, Green Lane Mill,
Holmfirth, West Yorkshire,
England, HD9 2DX
Email: urbanstreets@knitrowan.com
Internet: www.knitrowan.com

INFORMATION

Tension

Obtaining the correct tension is perhaps the single factor which can make the difference between a successful garment and a disastrous one. It controls both the shape and size of an article, so any variation, however slight, can distort the finished garment.
Different designers feature in our books and it is **their** tension, given at the **start** of each pattern, which you must match. We recommend that you knit a square in pattern and/or stocking stitch (depending on the pattern instructions) of perhaps 5 - 10 more stitches and 5 - 10 more rows than those given in the tension note. Mark out the central 10cm square with pins. If you have too many stitches to 10cm try again using thicker needles, if you have too few stitches to 10cm try again using finer needles. Once you have achieved the correct tension your garment will be knitted to the measurements indicated in the size diagram shown at the end of the pattern.

Sizing & Size Diagram Note

The instructions are given for the smallest size. Where they vary, work the figures in brackets for the larger sizes. **One set of figures refers to all sizes.** Included with most patterns in this brochure is a **'size diagram'**, or sketch of the finished garment and its dimensions. The size diagram shows the finished width of the garment at the under-arm point, and it is this measurement that the knitter should choose first; a useful tip is to measure one of your own garments which is a comfortable fit. Having chosen a size based on width, look at the corresponding length for that size; if you are not happy with the total length which we recommend, adjust your own garment before beginning your armhole shaping - any adjustment after this point will mean that your sleeve will not fit into your garment easily - don't forget to take your adjustment into account if there is any side seam shaping. Finally, look at the sleeve length; the size diagram shows the finished sleeve measurement, taking into account any top-arm insertion length. Measure your body between the centre of your neck and your wrist, this measurement should correspond to half the garment width plus the sleeve length. Again, your sleeve length may be adjusted, but remember to take into consideration your sleeve increases if you do adjust the length - you must increase more frequently than the pattern states to shorten your sleeve, less frequently to lengthen it.

Chart Note

Each square on a chart represents a stitch and each line of squares a row of knitting. Each colour used is given a different letter and these are shown in the **materials** section, or in the **key** alongside the chart of each pattern. When working from the charts, read odd rows (K) from right to left and even rows (P) from left to right, unless otherwise stated.

Knitting With Colour

There are two main methods of working colour into a knitted fabric: **Intarsia** and **Fairisle** techniques. The first method produces a single thickness of fabric and is usually used where a colour is only required in a particular area of a row and does not form a repeating pattern across the row, as in the fairisle technique.
Intarsia: The simplest way to do this is to cut short lengths of yarn for each motif or block of colour used in a row. Then joining in the various colours at the appropriate point on the row, link one colour to the next by twisting them around each other where they meet on the wrong side to avoid gaps. All ends can then either be darned along the colour join lines, as each motif is completed or then can be " knitted-in" to the fabric of the knitting as each colour is worked into the pattern. This is done in much the same way as"weaving- in" yarns when working the Fairisle technique and does save time darning-in ends. It is essential that the tension is noted for **Intarsia** as this may vary from the stocking stitch if both are used in the same pattern.
Fairisle type knitting: When two or three colours are worked repeatedly across a row, strand the yarn **not** in use loosely behind the stitches being worked. If you are working with more than two colours, treat the "floating" yarns as if they were one yarn and always spread the stitches to their correct width to keep them elastic. It is advisable not to carry the stranded or "floating" yarns over more than three stitches at a time, but to weave them under and over the colour you are working. The "floating" yarns are therefore caught at the back of the work.

Finishing Instructions

After working for hours knitting a garment, it seems a great pity that many garments are spoiled because such little care is taken in the pressing and finishing process. Follow the following tips for a truly professional-looking garment.

Pressing

Block out each piece of knitting and following the instructions on the ball band press the garment pieces, omitting the ribs. Tip: Take special care to press the edges, as this will make sewing up both easier and neater. If the ball band indicates that the fabric is not to be pressed, then covering the blocked out fabric with a damp white cotton cloth and leaving it to stand will have the desired effect. Darn in all ends neatly along the selvage edge or a colour join, as appropriate.

Stitching

When stitching the pieces together, remember to match areas of colour and texture very carefully where they meet. Use a seam stitch such as back stitch or mattress stitch for all main knitting seams and join all ribs and neckband with mattress stitch, unless otherwise stated.

Construction

Having completed the pattern instructions, join left shoulder and neckband seams as detailed above. Sew the top of the sleeve to the body of the garment using the method detailed in the pattern, referring to the appropriate guide:
Shallow set-in sleeves: Match decreases at beg of armhole shaping to decreases at top of sleeve. Sew sleeve head into armhole, easing in shapings.
Set- in sleeves: Place centre of cast-off edge of sleeve to shoulder seam. Set in sleeve, easing sleeve head into armhole.
Straight cast off: Place centre of cast- off edge of sleeve to shoulder seam. Sew top of sleeve to body.

Join side and sleeve seams.
Slip stitch pocket edgings and linings into place.
Sew on buttons to correspond with buttonholes.
Ribbed welts and neckbands and any areas of garter stitch should not be pressed.

Chain stitch

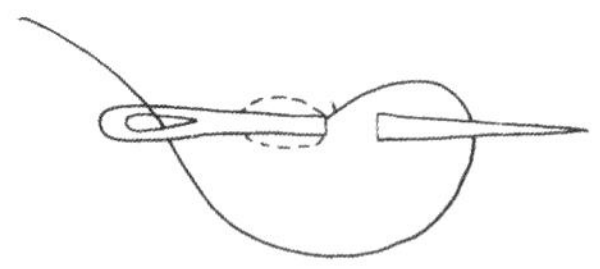

ABBREVIATIONS

K	knit
P	purl
st(s)	stitch(es)
inc	increas(e)(ing)
dec	decreas(e)(ing)
st st	stocking stitch (1 row K, 1 row P)
g st	garter stitch (K every row)
beg	begin(ning)
foll	following
rem	remain(ing)
rev st st	reverse stocking stitch (1 row P, 1 row K)
rep	repeat
alt	alternate
cont	continue
patt	pattern
tog	together
mm	millimetres
cm	centimetres
in(s)	inch(es)
RS	right side
WS	wrong side
sl 1	slip one stitch
psso	pass slipped stitch over
tbl	through back of loop
M1	make one stitch by picking up horizontal loop before next st and working into the back of it
yrn	yarn round needle
yfwd	yarn forward
meas	measures
0	no stitches, times or rows
-	no stitches, times or rows for that size
approx	approximately

EXPERIENCE RATINGS

 Easy, straight forward knitting / crocheting

 Suitable for the average knitter / crocheter

 For the more experienced knitter / crocheter

Photographer Gisela Torres • Stylist Emma Freemantle • Hair & Make-up Carol Morley • Model Bridget Amofah
Design Layout Simon Wagstaff

 Yarn quantities are approximate as they are based on average requirements.
Colour reproduction is as close as printing will allow.
First published in Great Britain in 2005 by Rowan Yarns Ltd, Green Lane Mill, Holmfirth, West Yorkshire, England, HD9 2DX
Internet: www.knitrowan.com Email: urbanstreets@knitrowan.com

British Library Cataloguing in Publication Data Rowan Yarns - Urban Streets
ISBN 1-904485-44-8